SHORT CUTS

INTRODUCTIONS TO FILM STUDIES

THE MUSICAL

RACE, GENDER AND PERFORMANCE

SUSAN SMITH

WALLFLOWER

LONDON and NEW YORK

A Wallflower Paperback

First published in Great Britain in 2005 by
Wallflower Press
6a Middleton Place, Langham Street, London W1W 7TE
www.wallflowerpress.co.uk

A catalogue record for this book is available from the British Library

ISBN 1 904764 37 1

Book Design by Rob Bowden Design

Printed in Great Britain by Antony Rowe Ltd, Chippenham, Wiltshire

CONTENTS

INTRODUCTION

As a film genre that was born out of the arrival of sound in movies and which went on to become one of the most successful mainstays of production during the studio system era, the Hollywood musical has, despite the many challenges that it has faced both industrially and culturally in the post-studio, post-classical period, continued to evolve and endure as an important and much loved area of American cinema. At the time that this book goes to print, the genre is poised at another fascinating point in its history as its flourishing partnership with the American animated film is now complemented by signs of a renewed viability and adaptability in the field of live-action cinema and as it is faced with the challenge of responding to the changing tastes and landscape of contemporary American music, not to mention the growing popularity in the Western world of alternative musical forms such as the Hindi musical. And all of this takes place against the backdrop of a growing rise in the DVD and 'home cinema' market, the technological advancements of which seem particularly well-suited to maximising the pleasures offered by a genre so rooted in the dynamics of music and song and the visual spectacle of the production number. The growing number of high-quality transfers of older (as well as new) musicals onto DVD has, of course, done much to reinvigorate our experience and appreciation of these films, enabling us to watch them in something like their original theatrical release format, while the special features available through the DVD remote handset have also opened up the possibility of audiences reorganising and redefining the ways in which they engage with the musical film text. The ability to skip effortlessly from one chapter of a film to another is one such feature, providing the viewer with the opportunity to move from number to number in ways that are able to by-pass the narrative sections of the film altogether, while the option to repeat an individual chapter or sequence *ad infinitum* may even allow for a more intense, perhaps obsessive engagement with a particular song or dance routine. The inclusion on certain DVD releases of a special feature that enables the viewer to sing along to the songs 'karaoke style' as the lyrics appear in time to the music at the bottom of the screen also constitutes an interesting attempt to overcome some of the difficulties that have been associated with the film musical on account of its status as a mechanical, recorded (rather than live) form of entertainment (on the latter see Altman (1987) and Feuer (1993)).

The advent of DVD and the increasing availability of movies in this format have therefore done much to heighten and foreground the pleasures and meanings that are to be derived from an engagement with the individual musical film text, the detailed elements of which, while always absolutely central to the popularity and significance of the genre, have, in academic terms, often been obscured by some of the more general theoretical and historical approaches that have been applied to it in the past. Yet on turning to the body of academic work that has been written on the musical, it is possible to detect signs (especially in recent years) of a move away from the kind of broad-based (mainly narrative and/or studio-centred) accounts that one associates with the traditional era of genre studies (key examples of which include the structuralist-influenced work of Altman (1987) and Feuer (1993)) in favour of studies devoted to the particularities of music, stars and individual films (see, for example, Marshall & Stilwell 2000; Gallafent 2000; Babington & Evans 1985). Yet how the specific properties and distinctive qualities of the musical come to shape our experience and understanding of individual texts still remains an area in need of much further exploration.

This book seeks to contribute to the advancement of such research by focusing on the central role played by performance (and other related elements) in the Hollywood musical. In doing so, it will offer close readings of particular moments of performance, examining how these operate within their given musical and narrative contexts, while also exploring how certain aspects of performance such as the singing voice can function across a range of films. By combining this kind of close reading approach with an interest in how the musical has utilised performance as a form of social role playing, this study seeks to address, in turn, the important contribution that performance has made in shaping and challenging the genre's treatment of race and gender, thereby bringing together under the umbrella of one book aspects of the musical that, while crucial and interlocking, have rarely been the subject of integrated analysis. In tackling some areas, consideration will be given to the ways in which the heightened mode of performance associated with the production number on the one hand renders the genre prone to offering highly amplified, ritualised enactments of racial and gender roles (with the artifice and theatricality of the elaborately staged, spectacular number lending itself particularly to this purpose), while at the same time providing opportunities for the development of more distinctive, creative forms of cultural and self-expression. Although the first of these tendencies is, as we shall see, more liable to be put to conservative, reactionary use, the study will examine instances of where, in more sensitive filmmaking hands, it can yield surprisingly interesting results. Indeed, as an example of how a musical may exploit the progressive possibilities arising from *both* such tendencies to musical performance, *The Pirate* (Vincente Minnelli, 1948) offers an excellent point of illustration here for, as various critics have observed, this is a film that demonstrates an ability to combine a more sophisticated, self-conscious interest in the socially performative nature of gender roles with a commitment to using musical performance (and the creativity and freedom of self-expression it can afford) as a way of gaining release from gender forms of entrapment (on these aspects, see Feuer 1993: 142; Wood 1986: 7; and Dyer 1986: 182–6).

While this book seeks to achieve a degree of balance when considering how the musical's handling of performance has contributed both to the disappointments and achievements of the genre where matters of race and gender are concerned, it is the more progressive possibilities arising from its various uses that will form the main focus of analysis. Chapter 1 therefore begins by critically evaluating some of the ways in which blackface performance – as a white racist form of racial masquerade and role-playing – has been understood to influence the Hollywood musical, before going on to explore the possibility of individual films displaying both a greater sensitivity to the performative nature of racial (and gender) roles and a more creative, progressive use of black and other forms of musical performance.

Chapter 2 is structured in terms of a similar dialectic as it begins by assessing how certain forms of musical spectacle have often been seen as implicating women in the performance of various gender stereotypes before going on to consider the more disruptive possibilities arising from the genre's use of the female voice. In exploring the importance of the female voice – especially the female singing voice – the book thus seeks to address what it considers to be one of the most vitally interesting yet neglected areas of both performance and the Hollywood musical as a whole. Because of the importance of the female singer to this part of the study, particular emphasis will be placed on the use of this figure in the 'backstage musical' sub-genre although, that said, we will also be addressing the significance of the speaking (not just singing) voice in musicals such as *My Fair Lady* (George Cukor, 1964) as well as the crucial role played by generic hybridity in articulating various gender-related tensions and concerns.

In adopting this kind of approach, the study in turn seeks to combine a critical evaluation of some of the key debates and arguments relating to race and gender in the Hollywood musical with a fresh, original analysis of how performance and other elements may function within the films themselves. Although a full analysis of the historical and cultural factors affecting both the development and reception of the kind of musical/performance styles used within these films lies outside the scope of this book, it is hoped that the conceptual framework provided at the beginning of the chapters will give the reader a sense of some of the most important work that has been carried out in these and other areas of the field and that they will be able to further explore them using the bibliography provided at the end of the book as a guide. As well as encouraging readers to engage in further reading and research on this topic, it is hoped, above all, that this study will help stimulate yet more close analysis of the films themselves – especially those areas that, as in the case of music and performance, are so central to the vitality of the genre and its ongoing significance and appeal.

1   RACE AND UTOPIA

Controlling black performance: strategies of exclusion and containment

Of the various strands of work that have dealt with the subject of race in the Hollywood musical (some of which form part of much wider race-related studies), a great deal of concern has centred on the ways in which the musical (and, in some cases, American cinema more broadly) has subjected black and other non-white performers to various strategies of exclusion and containment, while at the same time appropriating their musical styles and performing traditions for use by the dominant mainstream culture. In demonstrating such tendencies, this work has frequently centred on the genre's recourse to an earlier tradition of performance known as blackface, the practice of which was carried over into Hollywood cinema from the minstrel show.

As a form of popular entertainment that was fundamentally based on the exclusion and appropriation of black performers and black musical influences respectively, blackface minstrelsy had its roots in the days of slavery when African Americans were prevented by law from appearing on stage. This encouraged practices of white imitation and white caricature of black culture as white performers adopted the practice of blacking up their own faces with burnt cork and performing on stage the kinds of songs and dances they had learnt from black slaves. As Jacqui Malone observes: 'By the early 1800s, not long after the colonies declared their independence from England, white men were carrying their versions of slave dances to the American minstrel stage' (1996: 50). She goes on to say that 'from the 1840s through the 1890s, minstrel shows – wherein white men in blackface portrayed caricatures of black Americans and of black African American song and dance styles – were the most widespread form of American entertainment' (1996: 51). According to Malone, the minstrel show tended to play upon two basic Negro stereotypes – that of the 'shuffling old plantation slave' (usually portrayed as a happy, lazy, somewhat simple figure) and, as blacks gained their freedom and moved from the country to the city to gain work, that of the 'city dandy' (a stereotype designed to undermine the well-dressed, more affluent black) (ibid.).

When freed blacks were eventually allowed to perform on stage in minstrel shows after the Civil War they, too, were obliged to appear in blackface. This requirement for self-parody extended beyond the practice of 'applying burnt cork to their faces and painting red gaping mouths over their lips' (Hill 2000: 88) to an adoption of fake Negro dialects and the standard stereotypes mentioned above. Yet while the minstrel show eventually implicated African American performers themselves in these white caricatures of black people and black culture, it did at least provide a vital showcase for their talents. As a result, black performers managed to revitalise and challenge the stereotyped conventions of the minstrel show format through the introduction of more genuine forms of African American music and dance. Indeed, as Michael Rogin observes, 'they pushed the form as far in the direction of African American self-expression as it could go' (1996: 44). As Thomas Riis also points out, blackface functioned very differently for black as opposed to white performers, providing a variation upon the mask worn by slaves for their white owners and enabling African American performers to 'show the white minstrel audiences what they wanted them to see' (Riis quoted in Malone 1996: 56). For Malone, 'No doubt part of the appeal, too, lay in this use of the minstrel mask as a cover for the expression of dissatisfaction and anger' (ibid.).

In the case of white performers, moreover, the minstrel mask has also been understood to function in more complex terms, serving not just as a form of ridicule but as a means of gaining access to supposedly 'black' qualities. As Constance Valis Hill observes, 'the blackface mask effected a closeness, an intimacy with "blackness", for it held the key to white imagined fantasies of what blacks possessed – spontaneity, carefree ease, happy-go-lucky charm, childlike innocence and a natural vitality' (2000: 92). The significance of blackface was further complicated by the fact that

many of the white performers who put on burnt cork were European immigrants who were themselves in danger of being stigmatised as racially
different. For these performers, the minstrel mask became, in its role as
a signifier of America's most popular form of mass entertainment at that
time, a means of gaining cultural acceptance, the irony being, of course,
that such a process of assimilation into the white mainstream could only
be achieved through a grotesque parody of black culture. As Peter Stanfield describes:

> In nineteenth-century minstrelsy the disguise of burnt cork permit-
> ted European immigrant cultures to find a common language in
> their shared whiteness formed out of the negative construction of
> blackness. Blackface had acted as a syncretic form where ethnic
> markers such as Irish dance, Alpine yodelling, Shakespeare,
> Polish polkas and Italian opera would be performed through the
> Americanising mask of burnt cork. (2000: 148)

And it is precisely this process of achieving assimilation through the mask
of blackface that Rogin traces in Hollywood's very first musical, *The Jazz
Singer* (Alan Crosland, 1927), a film that is also a notable landmark, of
course, in terms of the coming of sound. Centring on the story of Jakie
Rabinowitz (Al Jolson), the son of Jewish immigrant parents who wants
more than anything else to become a jazz singer, the film charts with
unusual explicitness the process by which one particular ethnic group
– the European immigrant Jew – sought to achieve integration in American
society (on this, see also Mulvey 1999: 18). The problems and tensions
that this process involves are expressed in terms of the inter-generational
conflict that arises between Jakie and his cantor father who, refusing to
embrace the popular music of America, instead expects his son to continue the family tradition of singing at the local synagogue. It is a conflict
between Old and New World identities that, as Rogin demonstrates in his
analysis of the film's oscillation between silent and sound passages, also
becomes intricately bound up with the dilemma facing cinema itself as
it hovered, at this transitional point in *its* history, between two different
technological formats. Commenting on the film's portrayal of the Jewish
immigrant experience, Rogin acknowledges how, by charting Jakie's
resulting estrangement from his father, the latter's death from a broken

heart and the son's eventual relinquishment of his role as successor to his father as cantor in the local synagogue, the film manages to 'depict the costs of assimilation to family and immigrant community alike, as well as the threat of self-obliteration faced by the son' (1996: 86).

But for Rogin, the main cost of assimilation is borne by blacks whose music and image are both appropriated in the service of this 'American-isation' of the son of an immigrant Jew. Above all, he argues, it is Jolson's performance in blackface – first during a critical moment in this charac-ter's identity crisis (when he is forced to choose between going on for the opening night of his show or standing in for his dying father as cantor at the synagogue) and then during the final musical number (where his sing-ing the song 'Mammy' on Broadway marks his successful assimilation into mainstream culture by the end of the film) – that enables him to make the transition from immigrant Jew to white American. Commenting upon the attraction of blackface for Jewish entertainers in the early 1900s, Rogin argues that while the minstrel mask did function on one level as a means of identification – enabling immigrant Jews to express their experience of persecution in Europe through the mask of another racially stigmatised group – it also served more importantly and quite differently as a way of *hiding* their Jewish identity behind this mask of blackness. By donning the burnt cork, the Jewish Jolson character is thus able, according to this logic, to efface his ethnic difference by drawing attention to the whiteness that lies underneath: 'I am not really black, underneath the burnt cork is white skin' (1996: 103). According to Rogin, then, assimilation by the immigrant Jew into white mainstream culture is only achieved through the racial sub-ordination and exclusion of blacks:

> Assimilation is achieved via the mask of the most segregated; the blackface that offers Jews mobility keeps the blacks fixed in place. By wiping out all difference except black and white, blackface turns Rabinowitz into Robin, but the fundamental binary opposition nev-ertheless remains. That segregation, imposed on blacks, silences their voices and sings in their name. Replacing the Old World Jew blackface also replaced the black. (1996: 112)[1]

Although *The Jazz Singer* is often seen as heralding the end of the black-face practice in mainstream American cinema (the idea being that the greater sense of realism offered by sound jarred with the obvious artifice of blackface performance), Rogin argues that the film demonstrated how the musical genre could in fact give new life to blackface minstrelsy which found a continued outlet in the 'non-realist', emotionally heightened, gestural mode of the production number. In doing so, *The Jazz Singer* also anticipates the way in which the Hollywood musical would use blackface as a form of 'self-reflexive celebration of American entertainment itself', serving as a means by which this genre would acknowledge 'Hollywood's roots in the first American mass entertainment form' (1996: 167). However, Rogin points out that even the self-reflexive musical eventually sought to efface its roots in minstrelsy as blackface became increasingly problematic during the era of black civil rights movements in America (1996: 195–8).

While Stanfield has also explained Hollywood's overall use of blackface in terms of its wish to provide a nostalgic evocation of an earlier vernacular tradition in American entertainment, he regards *The Jazz Singer* as quite untypical of the ways in which American cinema simultaneously and contradictorily sought to distance itself from blackface and what it represents:

> Set in the present and ending with Jolson's character in blackface, the film contravenes Hollywood's typical presentation of minstrelsy as a discrete performance or as a means to represent America's theatrical and musical past. (2000: 147)

Instead, Stanfield finds a more representative use of blackface in *Show Boat* (James Whale, 1936), the second of three film versions of the landmark musical play (first premiered on Broadway in 1927 and itself based on Edna Ferber's 1926 novel) about life on a Mississippi showboat known as the 'Cotton Blossom', a floating theatre dedicated to the performance of plays and minstrel-style acts. For Stanfield, *Show Boat* is more representative than *The Jazz Singer* because of the way that 'it begins in the past with the heroine performing in blackface and ends in the present when she has long since left behind the mask of burnt cork' (ibid.). As a result, blackface is used not just 'as a sign of a theatrical past, but ... also [as] a marker against which the characters are able to judge their social progress' (2000: 149):

Like so many of Hollywood's representations of America's past, *Showboat* shows how America has progressed from vulgar beginnings to a refined present. The vulgar is imagined as belonging to a vernacular American culture. Through the means of song, dance and dialect the vernacular is signified as black. Sometimes this is achieved through the mask of blackface, but more often without the mask. Black American culture, mediated through blackface, is, I argue, a consistent signifier of an American vernacular. (2000: 147–8)

As well as stressing how this positioning of blackface performances back in the past serves as a crucial means by which the film seeks to establish a distance between what it presents as a more refined, present-day America (construed as 'white') and the country's more 'vulgar beginnings' (construed as 'black'), Stanfield argues that the use of African American actors like Paul Robeson and Hattie McDaniel in secondary roles further reinforces this sense of separation between white and black. Their presence, he maintains, 'distances the white actors from the images of blackness they assume by blacking up, through emphasising the performance's artificiality and fabrication', all of which 'in turn naturalises the minstrel types the African American actors have assumed' (2000: 149). If one accepts Stanfield's reading of *Show Boat* (and see my response to it later on in this section), then it is possible to see the film enacting what Tara McPherson refers to in her book *Reconstructing Dixie* as a shift during the course of the last century from overt to covert modes of representing racial difference in narratives about the American South. She points out that 'whereas early twentieth-century [i.e. overt] racial logics tended to delineate whiteness in sharp contrast to blackness, by mid-century other [i.e. covert] modes of framing whiteness were developing, modes that tended to repress the relations between white and black' (2003: 7). The key difference here, she argues, is that 'the former brings together figurations of racial difference in order to fix the categories whereas the latter enacts a separation that nonetheless achieves a similar end' (2003: 25). In terms of *Show Boat*, 'the attempt [in response to 'the potential for racial confusion' arising from the use of blackface and a mixed racial cast] to keep a sense of dramatic separation between representations of white and black' (Stanfield 2000: 149) has the effect of reinforcing, on this reading, the very notion of racial segregation that elsewhere the film seems so intent on criticising through its sympathetic portrayal of the suffering caused to the mulatto figure Julie (Helen Morgan) by society's intolerance of her mixed racial identity.

In suggesting how the film reinforces the African American actors' association with certain minstrel-type roles, Stanfield's reading of *Show Boat* displays some affinity with Donald Bogle's work. Central to Bogle's argument is the notion that, while the sound era provided black actors with more opportunities to appear on screen (following the outmoding of the silent era practice whereby Negro roles would be performed by white actors in blackface), they were, nevertheless, expected to assume the same kind of racially stereotyped roles that silent cinema (drawing upon minstrely) had used. Arguing that these stereotypes underpin the portrayal of blacks in American cinema more broadly, he categorises these in the following terms: the 'Uncle Tom' figure (the Good Negro character, stoical, selfless and submissive, who never rebels); the 'Coon' ('the Negro as amusement object and black buffoon'); the tragic mulatto (a figure, like Julie in *Show Boat*, of mixed racial blood); the 'Mammy' (noted for her 'fierce independence. She is usually big, fat and cantankerous', a more religious 'tom-like' version of which he describes as the 'aunt jemima' figure); and, finally, the 'black buck' (often associated with a dangerous, overcharged sexuality) (1994: 7–13).

In terms of musical performers, Bogle cites the tap dancer Bill 'Bojangles' Robinson (one of the most important figures in the history of tap) as an example of how extremely talented black performers often fell victim to racial stereotyping. In Robinson's case, this usually involved being cast in 'Uncle Tom' roles, most archetypally of all in the films he made with child star Shirley Temple where he often played the role of servant in a white household. By pairing Robinson with a child female star – that is, by not giving him the equivalent of an adult female romantic partner like, say, Ginger Rogers (as Fred Astaire had been allowed) – Bogle also argues that Robinson was effectively rendered somewhat childlike himself and, as a result, 'de-sexed or sexually neutralised' on film (quote taken from the television documentary *Fascinatin' Rhythm*, 2001). Indeed, as he wryly observes, 'Theirs was the perfect interracial love match. For surely nothing would come of it' (1994: 47). While acknowledging the subversive power of certain performers (in the case of Bill Robinson's films with Shirley Temple, for example, he notes how 'Robinson became the master in their relationship when he taught her the staircase dance routines' (ibid.)), Bogle argues that only the most talented black actors have been able to overcome – through the force and charisma of their personality – what he refers to as 'the blackface fixation' in American cinema. Commenting upon the first all-black musical, *Hearts in Dixie* (Paul Sloane, 1929), Bogle defines this syndrome in the following terms:

> Directed by whites in scripts authored by whites and then photographed, dressed and made up by whites, the Negro actor, like the slaves he portrayed, aimed (and still does aim) always to please the master figure. To do so, he gives not a performance of his own, not one in which he interprets black life but one in which he presents for mass consumption black life as seen through the eyes of white artists. The actor becomes a black man in blackface. In almost every all-black spectacle to follow ... most of the actors suffered from the blackface fixation. Only the very gifted, very talented have overcome it. (1994: 27)

In an article that bears some strong connections with Bogle's work, Richard Dyer has broadened the scope of the debate, exploring the ways in which black performance in the Hollywood musical has been restricted not only by the containment of African American performers in racially stereotyped roles but by a limiting of their access to the utopian spaces of the musical world. Arguing that black and white performers have tended to have very different relations to such spaces, he claims that whereas blacks have typically been contained within 'one kind of ghetto or another – the all-black musical ... the number that can be chopped without disrupting either the story or the editing ... or, in the case of the sublime Bill Robinson, kiddies' corner squiring with Shirley Temple' (2000: 24–5), 'whites in musicals have a rapturous relationship with their environment' (2000: 28), enjoying a freedom to expand out into space, 'dancing wherever they want, singing as loudly or as intimately as they need' (2000: 26). While acknowledging that even white performers may be subject to certain generic forms of containment (for example, through the convention of locating performances within a theatre), he argues that the MGM-style musical is notable precisely for its tendency 'to break away from exclusive

show-within-a-show presentation, to give us singing in the rain and dancing in the street' and points out that this 'transition from a more confined
to a more open space' is a freedom that tends to be enjoyed exclusively
by whites: 'Black people doing the same would in the white imagination
seem like a terrifying attempt to take over' (ibid.). So if the ability to burst
out into song and dance whenever and wherever one likes constitutes one
of the fundamental pleasures of the genre then, according to Dyer, 'Where
the musical most disturbingly constructs a vision of race is in the fact that
it is whites' privilege to be able to do this, and what that tells us about the
white dream of being in the world' (2000: 25).

Viewed collectively, such approaches have sobering implications for
our understanding of the musical's utopian vision. For if the genre's utopianism depends, as Dyer argues in his seminal article 'Entertainment and
Utopia', upon its ability to 'offer the image of "something better" to escape
into, or something we want deeply that our day-to-day lives don't provide'
(1981: 177), then what the accounts reviewed here suggest is that the musical is unable to imagine its fantasies of escape in ways that do not end up
reproducing – or at least being severely compromised by – existing social
structures and hierarchies of white power, thereby perpetuating, in the
process, the very forms of racial oppression and unfreedom to which the
musical seems, in principle, so well suited to respond. Yet while the dis-
criminatory practices in Hollywood and beyond have undoubtedly shaped
the racial character of the musical in ways that have served to privilege
white needs, there is a danger, in focusing so exclusively on the whiteness
of the genre's spaces or on the pervasive hold of the 'blackface fixation' (to
use Bogle's term), of excluding from consideration other important dimen-
sions and other more progressive strands to the musical.

Strains of resistance: looking beyond the blackface fixation

As Kenneth MacKinnon has observed in his thoughtful response to Dyer's
article 'The Colour of Entertainment', an emphasis on the whiteness of
the musical's spaces may overlook the 'cruciality' of the genre's 'wishfulness' (2000: 40). Noting the irony with which he is able to counter Dyer's
reading here by drawing on this same critic's earlier article 'Entertainment
and Utopia', MacKinnon argues that a concentration on the spatial
dimension may neglect the way in which 'the utopianism of the musical

is expressed in feeling' (2000: 45) rather than in terms of some concrete, visually realisable space or form. As he points out, the hopes, dreams and fantasies of escape generated during the numbers often far exceed what the musical film is able to actualise or fulfil through the narrative spaces and solutions on offer within its fictional world, the intensity of feeling produced during such moments tending to encourage the belief in a utopian realm that lies somewhere just beyond the boundaries of the musical's diegetic world: 'It is the fervency of the belief in that utopia, together with the poignancy of its unattainability, that resonates in the experience of the genre's devotees' (2000: 46). In a reading that also demonstrates how matters of audience reception may further complicate our understanding of the racial character of the Hollywood musical, MacKinnon argues that it is this complex, ambivalent structure of feeling which lies at the heart of the musical's appeal to socially marginalised or oppressed groups:

> Minorities unaddressed in the overt content of musicals recognise in the longings and absences an appeal to their experience ... In their glimpses of discontent with prevailing social structures and the passion of the conviction with which a better place is fantasised, musicals can speak of oppression and speak to the oppressed, whether that speech is a force for quietism or radical change. The space of musicals may on one reading be white. A more spellbound reading could, though, occasion colour blindness. (2000: 45–6)

In the case of the other approaches considered above, an exclusive preoccupation with the blackface legacy may also encourage a highly deterministic reading, one that is prone to read Hollywood as fundamentally and inevitably conditioned by this racist parentage. In the case of Rogin's work, this is evident in the way that he tends to select films not for their ability to break away from the blackface tradition but, rather, for their capacity to demonstrate, in more explicit terms, what he argues other more 'run-of-the-mill' films typically try to hide – America's ingrained roots in blackface minstrelsy: 'When American film takes its great leaps forward, it returns to its buried origins. Then it exposes the cinematic foundations of American freedom in American slavery' (1996: 16). One possible implication of Rogin's argument is that any film or musical that does not acknowledge these 'buried origins' is liable to be construed as guilty of attempting to efface or deny (rather than reject) these blackface roots. Hence in his discussion of *Singin' in the Rain* (Gene Kelly and Stanley Donen, 1952), a self-reflexive musical about the coming of sound, Rogin argues that it attempts (unlike *The Jazz Singer*) to bury or hide its blackface origins by foregrounding instead the conflict between Lina Lamont and Kathy Selden (1996: 205). He also contends that *Singin' in the Rain* uses its thematic concern with the theft of the younger woman's voice to 'distract attention from the actual source of the film's greatness, its black inflected dance spectacles'. Thus, 'just as *The Jazz Singer* appropriated African American music, so *Singin' in the Rain* steals African American dance' (1996: 206).

While Bogle is perhaps more keen to acknowledge the possibility of certain performers exceeding the limits of their blackface roles, his discussion of such performances and what they involve remains frustratingly brief and tends, by and large, to confine itself to the level of the individual performer: the likelihood of a *film* employing its visual, aural and narrative strategies in ways that contest, rather than merely reinforce, the racial stereotyping in play is something that his approach is less well suited to address. As we shall see later in this chapter, the limitations of Bogle's approach become evident in his discussion of the all-black musical *Cabin in the Sky* (Vincente Minnelli, 1943), the more complex and progressive aspects of which tend to get obscured in his attempt to slot this film – and its black performers – into a broader descriptive schema of racially stereotyped themes and roles. By considering black actors' work almost exclusively in relation to such a schema, this kind of approach may be in danger of subjecting the performers involved to another form of containment, refusing them, as it does, a more organic interrelationship with a film's overall strategies and concerns.

Stanfield's reading of the 1936 version of *Show Boat* is much more sophisticated in its analysis of certain narrative and musical elements. However, in focusing his discussion around the white female protagonist's use of blackface (only one instance of which is literal, the other two being implied), his approach does nonetheless exclude other important aspects from consideration. An attention to point of view strategies, for example, might lead one to consider the film's tendency to offer a more sensitive treatment of the black characters' own perspective at certain critical moments in the narrative. During the miscegenation scene, for example, its strategy of cutting away from the action to show Joe (Robeson) watching Julie's enforced departure from the boat (following the exposure of her mulatto status by the authorities) is crucial in helping to establish a more authentic black point of view on the situation. In his study of Paul Robeson's star persona in *Heavenly Bodies*, Dyer analyses this scene as an example of how 'Joe's emblematic presence is most called upon at specifically racially sensitive moments in the play and film' (1986: 127–8). Comparing Robeson's performance as Joe in the 1928 stage and 1936 film versions of *Show Boat*, Dyer notes how, during one of the cutaways (in the film) to a shot showing this character standing observing events from the balcony, Joe/Robeson is able to convey 'with one movement of his eyes and head … a wealth of unfathomable meaning' and concludes that 'the film, even more it would seem than the show, stresses Joe/Robeson as an emblem of racial suffering. Both staging and editing register awareness of racism in Robeson's passive observation of it' (1986: 128).

In his analysis of Robeson's performance of 'Old Man River' (a song which he refers to as a 'white man's spiritual' (1986: 87)), Dyer also examines how the singer sought to resist the white view of negro culture inherent in the lyrics by changing the words of the song so as 'to bring out and extend its reference to oppression and to alter its meaning from resignation to struggle' (1986: 105). While the most radical changes occurred in Robeson's later concert performances, Dyer traces the emergence of such tendencies from 1928 onwards (for example, '*Niggers* all work on *de* Mississippi' is changed to '*Darkies* all work on *the* Mississippi' (ibid.))[2] and argues that the effects of both this and the harsher references to 'white rule and the black man's hopeless lot' (ibid.) in the chorus section are magnified in the 1936 film version by the camera's strategy of framing Robeson in angry, labour-ridden poses during the expressionist montage sequence that occurs mid-way during the number (1986: 106).

Taking into account the more complex effects arising from these moments of performance and the film's foregrounding of them, it might therefore be possible to argue that while Robeson and his black co-star Hattie MacDaniel only appear in the first two thirds of the film, the effect of their presence when they are on screen manages to leave a lasting impression that counters the more racist effacement of their characters from the final section of the narrative, the force of their performances enabling them to stay in the cinematic memory long after the resolution of the white characters' dilemma in the closing sequence. And if a study of these particular instances of black performance and black point of view has highlighted a certain degree of resistance in the text to what Stanfield sees as the film's attempt to naturalise the African American actors in their minstrel type roles, then a fuller consideration of *Show Boat*'s thematic concerns might also lead us to construe the performances in blackface by Magnolia (Irene Dunne) as part of a more extensive and critical attempt by the film to associate the white characters with various kinds of artifice and pretence. The centrality of such practices to the white characters' everyday lives is made clear very early on when Captain Andy (Charles Winninger) is shown passing off the fight that takes place between Julie's husband and her jealous admirer as merely a piece of play-acting drawn from the show and put on for the diegetic audience's benefit. It is a strategy of pretence that not only enables him to preserve the illusion that the show business community is 'just one big happy family' but also serves (less intentionally on his part) to conceal the more serious tensions inherent in this romantic rivalry between the two men who (unlike the rest of the crew) are aware of Julie's mixed racial identity.

The white characters' association with pretence is developed most centrally of all, though, through the musical number 'Make Believe'. Sung as a romantic duet by Magnolia and Gaylord Ravenal (Allan Jones) on their first meeting, this number is crucial in enabling the film to foreground how the white characters' whole way of looking at the world is founded on a belief in the transformative power of illusion:

> Gaylord: Only make-believe I love you,
> Only make-believe that you love me.
> Others find peace of mind in pretending –
> Couldn't you?
> Couldn't I?
> Couldn't we?
> Make-believe our lips are blending
> In a phantom kiss, or two or three.
> Might as well make-believe I love you,
> For to tell the truth, I do.

Magnolia:	The game of just supposing
	Is the sweetest game I know.
	Our dreams are more romantic
	Than the world we see –
Gaylord:	And if the things we dream about
	Don't happen to be so,
	That's just an unimportant technicality.
Magnolia:	Though the cold and brutal fact is
	You and I have never met,
	We need not mind convention's 'P's and 'Q's.
	If we put our thoughts in practice
	We can banish all regret
	Imagining most anything we choose.
	We could make-believe I love you,
	We could make-believe that you love me.
Both:	Might as well make-believe I love you,
Gaylord:	For to tell the truth, I do.

The significance of this number heightens when one considers how, in singing about the power of 'Make Believe' to transform reality into something better, Magnolia and Gaylord give vent to the musical's own utopian vision (not to mention the illusion-making powers of Hollywood as a whole). Yet if this is something that the film partly seeks to endorse as, true to the lyrics of the song, Magnolia and Gaylord begin to fall in love as they sing the words to each other, then elsewhere it adopts a range of narrative and musical strategies that seem designed to throw this into question. Hence, as the romance between Magnolia and Gaylord unfolds, the film emphasises the illusoriness that underpins it by having the early stages of their relationship acted out on stage during their performances together in the play 'Tempest and Sunshine'. And in proceeding to show Gaylord abandoning his wife and child once his lucky gambling streak runs out and they hit hard times, the film reveals it to be a form of romance that the reality of their marriage is quite unable to sustain.

In more immediate terms, the decision to preserve the structure of the original Broadway stage production of *Show Boat* by positioning Paul Robeson's powerful rendition of the song 'Old Man River' so that it follows on directly after the 'Make Believe' number also has the effect of encouraging a degree of detachment from Magnolia and Gaylord and the kind of utopianism that they espouse. For while both songs express a certain wishfulness and a desire to evade reality, the emphasis on suffering and labour that is evident both in the lyrics of 'Old Man River' ('Darkies all work on the Mississippi, Darkies all work while the white folk play') and in the striking images of Robeson and the other blacks caught in various postures of heavy toil serves to make clear the much harsher realities facing the black people within the narrative world and thus the difficulty for them of indulging in any equivalent naive belief in the transformative powers of illusion. When considered within the context of this musical juxtaposition, the mood of resignation to black suffering that Dyer observes in 'Old Man River' arguably takes on a stronger political force, with such lines as 'I gets weary and sick of tryin', I'm tired of livin' and scared of dyin'' following on in stark contrast to the white characters' earlier complacent dismissal of social realities: 'Our dreams are more romantic/Than the world we see – And if the things we dream about/Don't happen to be so, *That's just an unimportant technicality.*'

If the force of this juxtaposition helps to critically foreground (rather than merely reinforce) what Dyer refers to elsewhere as the whiteness of the musical's utopian spaces then it is an ironic effect that can also be seen as extending beyond these numbers to other areas of the narrative. The white characters' assumptions about being able to dismiss and transform reality through the power of 'Make Believe' is especially at odds, the film implies, with what Julie experiences. In her case, the appearance of being white is construed, by the authorities' racist standards, as a form of pretence that most certainly *cannot* be tolerated, the disjuncture between how she would like to live her life and the racial discrimination to which she is subject clearly amounting to more than 'just an unimportant technicality'.

Music, image, narrative: a close analysis of the ending of Show Boat

One of the most interesting aspects to the MGM remake of *Show Boat* (George Sidney, 1951) is the way that it follows through some of the more critical tendencies arising from this musical juxtaposition of the songs 'Make Believe' and 'Old Man River'. In this case, though, the juxtaposition is withheld until the end of the film when (in an eschewal of the earlier film's problematic modern-day section depicting the successful stage career of Magnolia's grown up daughter), Gaylord (Howard Keel) is shown returning to the 'Cotton Blossom' following his discovery that he has a young daughter. In bringing the two songs together at the end, the film thus restores what it had earlier broken up through the relocation of William Warfield's first rendition of 'Old Man River' to the point in the narrative where Julie (Ava Gardner) is forced to leave the boat following the exposure of her mixed racial identity. On that occasion, the loss of ironic contrast produced by this shift was more than compensated for by the number's ability to offer a direct commentary on the racial injustice practiced within the narrative, with Robeson's silent black perspective on Julie's departure being re-placed in this instance by Warfield's stirring rendition of 'Old Man River'. In then restoring the musical juxtaposition of these two songs in the final scene, the film is able to develop the significance of the earlier version of the 'Only Make Believe' number while avoiding – through what is a major reprisal of the song 'Old Man River' – the narrative forgetting of the black characters that occurred in the 1936 version.

This relocation of the two songs to the end of the film does not come without its own form of ideological pressure, however. For in using the song 'Make Believe' to bring Gaylord closer to his daughter during their first meeting on the wharf and then having Joe/Warfield's second rendition of 'Old Man River' accompany Gaylord and Magnolia (Kathryn Grayson) as they return, now reconciled, to the boat, the film involves these numbers in a form of narrative resolution that clearly privileges the white characters' situation. In the case of 'Make Believe', the song allows Gaylord to express his feelings for his daughter under the cover of pretence: 'Could you make-believe that I was your daddy?' he asks Kim before taking her on his knee and singing a variation of the lyrics he had earlier sung to her mother: 'Only make-believe I'm near you, Only make-believe that you're with me.' Not only that but it also enables him to wipe away several years of paternal absence in one fell swoop: 'Darling, look. If your daddy really did come back, could you make-believe that – look, could you pretend that he'd never been away? Could you sweetheart?' he asks.

In the case of 'Old Man River', too, it is easy to see how its reprisal here works in support of Dyer's argument about the universalising tendencies inherent in this song. Having earlier acted as a very specific commentary upon the suffering and loss caused to Julie by the miscegenation ruling, it now seems to serve as a kind of emotional backdrop to the *white couple*'s reunion, the suffering alluded to in the song's lyrics thus being extended and reapplied to *their* trials and tribulations. In this sense, 'Old Man River' helps the film to perform an ideological manoeuvre similar to the one that took place mid-way through Warfield's first rendition of the song when, amid the racially charged atmosphere of Julie's departure, the music momentarily receded into the background just as Gaylord arrived to offer himself as the new leading man to replace Julie's husband. The switch from black to white, racial to romantic concerns that the Howard Keel character's arrival signified on that occasion is reflected in the shifting role played by the music. As Warfield stops singing and a chorus of black singers takes over in a quieter tone of voice, the song not only becomes musically subservient to this new narrative situation but also seems to undergo an actual transference of meaning: like the river, the show must 'just keep rolling along' it now seems to say.

Yet while the re-juxtaposition of these two songs at the end can be understood as acting, on one level, in the service of white needs, the overall effect created by the musical, performative and visual elements is arguably much more complex. This is evident first of all in the 'Make Believe' sequence which, rather than serving simply as an opportunity to reassert the white characters' confident belief in their ability to turn their dreams into reality, instead manages to highlight both the costs and inadequacy of this kind of outlook on life. The initial shot showing the little girl playing alone on the wharf with her two dolls encapsulates this more critical strand of meaning quite perfectly as it demonstrates how her absorption in her own game of make believe (she pretends that the dolls are her parents) requires her both to shut herself off from any more positive interaction with the group of black and white children playing around her ('We get away from those noisy people. We go asleep in the woods', she tells her dolls) and to construct an illusory notion of the family as a compensation for the reality of her situation. Rather than simply appearing as an innocent game of child-like pretence that will easily be outgrown, Kim's investment in 'make believe' is presented here as an ideological inheritance passed down from one white generation to the next and one that serves to lock the child herself into a self-contained fantasy world. And while Gaylord (like Kim) tries to use the power of 'make believe' to erase the years of paternal absence, his efforts are characterised by a sense of poignancy and strain, his awareness of the emotional loss that this game of pretence seeks to efface being indicated by the faltering nature of Keel's normally so robust vocal delivery and by the way that his character breaks down in tears before completing the final line of the song.

The use of 'Old Man River' to accompany Magnolia and Gaylord's return to the boat is also complicated by the way that Joe takes over from the chorus of singers mid-way through the number and begins to sing lines that, in their reference to the arduousness of black labour, resist easy assimilation into white needs. (In this sense, the number again provides a variation on that moment during the first rendition of the song when, having momentarily receded into the background in the manner referred to earlier, Joe/Warfield's singing strikes up powerfully once again as it resumes its more oppositional function as an empathetic voice of black commentary on Julie's suffering.) It is not just what Joe sings that is important here but the way that the music interacts with the film's visual elements. As he sings 'You and me, We sweat and strain, Body all achin' and racked with pain', the camera does not just follow the white couple as they move up towards the top deck of the boat but instead observes this from a more detached, low-angle viewpoint, its position on the main deck at the very point where Joe sings these words serving as a reminder of the song's association with the black workers' situation. As such, the words 'You and me' seem to function less as a way of effacing the specific conditions of black oppression by embracing whites and blacks in one generalising mode of address and more as a way of emphasising how different the black people's situation is from that of the white characters at this point in the film: indeed, Joe's words seem to constitute a very specific appeal to his fellow workers whose toils will continue beyond the point of narrative closure. This meaning is developed in the next shot where the image of Magnolia's parents congratulating themselves on their daughter's reunion with her husband is overlaid with the sound of Joe singing: 'Tote that barge and lift that bale...'.

By counter-pointing the image and music in this way, the film invites us to adopt an ironic distance from the white characters by making clear how their self-absorption in their own happy ending ('It's Saturday night forever!', Captain Andy (Joe E. Brown) exclaims gleefully in an earlier version of this same shot) renders them oblivious to the ongoing fact of black suffering. So despite the more specific ideological limitations of the lyrics of 'Old Man River', there are certain tensions arising from the use of this music in its present context that go some way towards disturbing and problematising the move towards narrative resolution. At times it opens up the possibility of an almost Brechtian-like distance from the white characters that enables us to recognise both the racially privileged nature of the happy ending that is on offer here and the white egocentric form of utopianism that it involves. The appearance of Julie at the wharf shortly afterwards reinforces this effect by highlighting (in a way that the 1936 version did not) how Magnolia's reconciliation with her husband is not matched by any corresponding resolution to her best friend's situation.

Focusing upon the musical elements in this way should not lead us to assume, however, that this version of *Show Boat* is radical in its overall treatment of race, the possibilities but also limits of which are suggested by one particular close-up showing the Ava Gardner character smiling and then blowing a kiss to the couple on the boat. In foregrounding her point of view at this crucial point, the film goes so far as to demonstrate a sensitivity to her exclusion on racial grounds (an awareness that is heightened by the song's ability to re-evoke the injustice of her earlier enforced departure from the boat) yet it does so in a way that reinforces her passive acceptance of her situation, as a self-sacrificing figure resigned to living out her desires vicariously through her white 'sister' Magnolia. Yet while the film is in certain respects quite conventional in its treatment of the *Show Boat* story, what this detailed analysis of the closing sequence has revealed is a capacity on the part of the musical elements to open up a more complex perspective than might otherwise be the case – one wherein the resolution of the white characters' situation (itself qualified by poignant feelings of loss) is countered by an ironic awareness of the black characters' inability to gain release from their suffering.

In offering both a more chastened reworking of the white characters' earlier complacent assertion of their belief in the world of 'Make Believe' and an extensive reminder of the ongoing fact of black suffering, the film's closing sequence therefore manages to produce an emotional texture that (in ways that seem quite different from the 'colonial structure of feeling' that Dyer identifies in the MGM style musical (2000: 27)) tends to qualify and complicate its investment in the couple's romantic reunion at the end. In doing so, the film manages to push the implications arising from the musical juxtaposition of 'Make Believe' and 'Old Man River' in the 1936 version of *Show Boat* a stage further and in a manner that enables it to more effectively challenge the kind of lenticular logic that Tara McPherson sees as afflicting and delimiting narrative representations of the American South:

> a schema by which histories or images that are actually co-present get presented (structurally, ideologically) so that only one of the images can be seen at a time. Such an arrangement represses connection, allowing whiteness to float free from blackness, denying the long historical imbrications of racial markers and racial meaning in the South. (2003: 7)

In the complex and at times contrapuntal relationship it establishes between the musical and visual elements in this final number, the 1951 version of *Show Boat* instead demonstrates how:

> Some narratives and images break free of such a limiting schema, refusing both the covert representations of the lenticular, as well as the more overt modes of an earlier period, fashioning new paradigms of vision and visibility and refusing the comforts of partition and separation. (2003: 7–8)

Strategies of subversion in Cabin in the Sky

This ability to problematise the racial assumptions underpinning the musical's utopian sensibility is something that we can explore much more extensively in relation to Vincente Minnelli's all-black musical *Cabin in the Sky*. As an example of a form of production that reflects 'the hypocritical, separate-but-equal policies of a segregated society' (Naremore 1993: 70), this is a film whose title would seem to signify a straightforward compliance with the racially conservative conventions of the musical genre, the 'cabin in the sky' ideal implying, in this case, not so much a complete exclusion of blacks from the utopian realms of the musical world as a white-imagined, white-caricatured view of what black people would want utopia to look like. Yet, as we shall see, there is an alternative coherence to the film's use of music and performance that enables it to express its utopian sensibility in much more racially progressive terms, the fulfilment of which is both heightened and complicated by its sensitive attention to gender concerns.

In arguing for such complexities in *Cabin in the Sky*,[3] the reading outlined here differs quite markedly from the kind adopted by Donald Bogle in his account of the film. Although Bogle goes so far as to acknowledge the quality of the all-star cast (at one point he says of Ethel Waters that: 'When she sang "Happiness is a Thing Called Joe", the fantasy world of *Cabin in the Sky* vanished and the reality of a strong, heartfelt experience entered' (1994: 129)), overall he tends to see the film as very much reproducing the racially stereotyped representations of negro life that he associates with earlier all-black productions:

> A light and ingratiating fantasy, *Cabin in the Sky* told the story of Little Joe Jackson, a harmless little coloured man who enjoys shooting craps and raising a bit of cain. He is married to a decent God-fearing woman, Petunia, who worries plenty about him. But neither Joe nor Petunia knows of the battle between the general of heaven and Lucifer, Jr. of hell for the rights to Jackson's soul. To win his victim, Lucifer, Jr., throws everything – including a winning sweepstakes ticket and the temptress Georgia Brown – Little Joe's way. But, in the end, Petunia's prayers save him, and together the two are able to walk to their cabin in the sky … In subject matter, *Cabin in the Sky* resembled earlier black films. Again, Negroes were removed from the daily routine of real American life and placed in a remote idealised world. As in the past, the exotic features of black existence were played up. There was the familiar theme of the Good Coloured Boy who leaves at home the Christian Good Woman to take up with the Bad Black Girl. And once more, as in *Green Pastures*, ersatz Negro folk culture was passed off as the real thing. (1994: 128–31)

If one were to accept this summary as a complete and accurate account of *Cabin in the Sky* then it certainly would be difficult to see the film as offering anything other than a naïve, unquestioning endorsement of the white caricatured notion of black utopia that is encapsulated in its title song. Performed early on in the dream section of the narrative during the scene where Joe (Eddie Anderson) is shown enjoying a picnic with his wife Petunia (Ethel Waters), this number is preceded by a brief conversation between the couple that begins with Joe expressing gratitude for all that Petunia has done for him during his (imagined) recuperation from the gunshot wound caused by his gambling-related fracas with Domino Johnson (John 'Bubbles' Sublett). On hearing Joe profess a desire to mend his ways, Petunia expresses her belief that he will stay reformed and, on being asked why, she explains her faith in her husband in religious terms, assuring him that: 'If we do the job right here, they won't let us down when we're finally ready to go home.' It is at this point that she begins to sing the title song, an extract from which is provided below:

> In this cloudy sky overhead now
> There's no guiding star I can see.
> And I would be lost,
> By each wild tempest tossed,
> Oh, if I didn't know
> Of a place we two can go.
> There's a little cabin in the sky, mister,
> For me and for you
> I feel that it's true somehow.
> Can't you see that cabin in the sky, mister?
> An acre or two of heavenly blue to plough.
> We will be, oh so gay,
> All we'll do is sing and pray,
> As the angels go sailing by.
> And that is why my heart is flying high, mister,
> 'Cos I know we'll have
> A cabin in the sky.

Perhaps the most folkloric scene in the entire film, it is not difficult to find elements in it that correspond with Bogle's account: the idealised rural setting; the group of happy blacks (dressed in a simple, rustic style of clothing) who gather around the couple and lend vocal support to Petunia's singing; the devoutness of Petunia's faith which enables her to justify and accept the hardship of her situation with cheerful patience; and, above all, the song's construction of her dream of heaven in terms that, by associating it with a state of rustic contentment and simplicity, serves to reinforce the lowliness of blacks in the social order. Yet to leave matters there would be to ignore several other elements relating to the performance of the song. Most crucial of all is Ethel Waters' singing voice, the sophistication of which tends to contest the simplicity of the rural idyll alluded to in the lyrics. Her injection of deep blues notes into lines such as 'Where we'll be, oh so gay, All we'll do is sing and pray' and the gospel-style rhythm and ornamentation that she brings to the final rendition of 'Cos I know we'll have, A cabin in the sky' (reinforced by the black chorus' emulation of her style of delivery in their interpolated response to the first of these lines) are particularly effective in evoking a more complex, authentic sense of black experience and black religious feeling than that embodied in the untroubled idealism of the words themselves. The effect of the song is further complicated by the contrapuntal use of Anderson's singing voice, the gravelly, 'earthy' texture of which (in struggling to reach the higher notes) helps reinforce his character's more explicit expressions of resistance to the utopian ideal: 'Cabin life may be sweet but it sounds so incomplete, I prefer my easy street right now. Since I guess I'll never learn to fly, lady, I'm just passing by that cabin in the sky.'

Along with these vocal elements, the narrative transition that occurs directly after this number to the 'Hotel Hades' scene also has the effect of further challenging any more straightforward affirmation of the 'cabin in the sky' ideal. By depicting hell both as a place filled with the creative, vibrant rhythms of jazz and as an outfit run along the lines of a Hollywood studio[4] where Bible stories are presented as fictional constructions made up as if for a film script by Lucifer Jr's 'Idea Men' (one of whom is played by Louis Armstrong), the film adopts a highly tongue-in-cheek approach to religion that strongly subverts the tone of what went before. It is a strategy that, in countering Petunia's own earnest investment in the 'cabin in the sky' ideal and in suggesting a quite ironic attitude towards the heaven = white/hell = black dichotomy that structures the story, demonstrates its capacity for establishing a much more complex relationship to its subject matter than what Bogle is prepared to allow for in his previously quoted account. As such, it also points to a concern on the part of the film with interrogating, rather than merely reproducing, the stereotypical conventions that Bogle associates with the all-black production.

In his book *The Films of Vincente Minnelli*, James Naremore is much more responsive to this tonal complexity in the film. Considering *Cabin in the Sky* within the context of a particularly important moment in the history of all-black Hollywood productions – 'when African Americans were increasing their demands for better treatment from the movie industry, and when the federal government was engaged in a semi-official drive to encourage pictures with black casts' (1993: 51) – he argues that the film's folkloric project (itself attributable, he suggests, to a more liberal strain than the kind to which Bogle refers) is countered or complicated by a 'strong feeling of urbanity and sophistication' (1993: 59). He relates this not just to the 'growing commodification and modernisation of American life' as a whole but to the influence of a 'cosmopolitan artistic sensibility' that, derived from Broadway and the European avant-garde, tended to promote images of a more 'chic, upscale' form of Africanism (ibid.). Arguing that this influence feeds into the film through its director Vincente Minnelli (who had just made the transition from Broadway to Hollywood), Naremore maintains that it is this figure who is responsible, above all, for '*Cabin in the Sky*'s distinctly urban tone' (1993: 60), the disruptive effect of which, in tending 'to undermine the conservative implications of the original material' (1993: 62) helps to set this film apart from its all-black predecessors.

However, while Naremore acknowledges the disruptions that the film's urban tone poses to its ostensible subject matter, he does so in a way that, often concentrating on Minnelli's tendency to use more elaborate, opulent forms of setting, decor and costuming than would ordinarily be found in a folkloric movie, ultimately tends to construe *Cabin in the Sky*'s progressiveness in fairly limited terms:

> [Arthur] Freed and Minnelli were hardly social activists, but by imbuing their film with a dreamy atmosphere and an urban Africanism, they and the performers turned it into what is arguably the most visually beautiful picture about black people ever produced at the classic studios. We might say that during the early 1940s in Hollywood, their aestheticism amounted to a modestly positive gesture. (1993: 70)

Yet one could go further and argue that a detailed analysis of the film's use of music and performance is likely to reveal a much deeper, more fully developed set of progressive concerns. With this in mind, let us focus on one particular number in close detail before moving on to consider the ways in which this musical unit relates to *Cabin in the Sky* as a whole. The number in question takes place midway through the dream narrative and is the one where Petunia sings 'Taking a Chance On Love' in the kitchen of her home following Joe's return from work and his surprise gift to her of an electric washing machine for her birthday. The gift of the electric washing machine is what actually helps to trigger the start of the number, in fact, for it is on seeing Petunia overcome with gratitude that Joe tries to lighten up the atmosphere by asking her to sing for him. As such, it provides a highly appropriate lead-in to the song,[5] on the one hand revealing an impulse on Joe's part to break free from the rustic simplicity of black cabin life (the primitive conditions of which are highlighted by his comment: 'Now all we need is some electricity so we can run it'), while at the same time enabling him to find some relief from his male anxieties through this extravagant display of his newfound earning power.

The gift's ability to embody certain wish-fulfilling male desires on Joe's part is reinforced by the way that, in his dream, he grants himself a more physically demanding job than the post of hotel lift operator that was referred to in the opening scene. The strenuous nature of his job at the local feed mill thereby provides him with the opportunity (just before he gives Petunia the washing machine) to show off his muscles and to boast about being the strongest man at work. And if the gift can be construed partly as an attempt, on Joe's part, to gain relief from the pressures of his breadwinner role then, significantly, it *also* carries with it a recognition of the oppressiveness of *Petunia*'s gender position, fulfilling as it does his earlier promise (made during the picnic scene) to relieve the Ethel Waters character of her domestic chores. And it is the modernising, emancipating potential of the gift in both racial and gender terms that the number itself is able to fulfil in much more creative, positive ways through its injection of various contemporary forms of music and dance into the cabin sphere.

For the purposes of analysis, the number can be divided into four main sections:

1   Petunia is persuaded to sing 'Taking a Chance on Love' by Joe who accompanies her on the guitar. Bill (Bill Bailey) also joins in by playing a harmonica-style instrument.

2 Bill moves into the kitchen and tap dances while Petunia continues to sing and Joe still plays the guitar.

3 Joe takes over from Bill by performing a comical dance routine around the kitchen, having passed the guitar over to the younger man. Petunia continues to stand near the doorway singing.

4 Joe and Petunia dance together. Petunia then bursts into a more energetic bout of song and dance, much to Joe's surprise. The number ends with Petunia singing the title line of the song again.

Before moving on to a detailed analysis of each section, it is important to begin by acknowledging the vital role played by the performances in producing a sense of diversity and individuality of expression that runs counter to the notion of racial stereotyping. It is not just the delightful contrasts between the three performing styles that count here but also the marked shifts and nuances that are to be found within the individual performances themselves. That is, in the tonal range of Ethel Waters'

vocal delivery, in the changing rhythms of Bill Bailey's taps, and in the comic detail of Eddie Anderson's facial expressions and bodily movements. There is also a sense of fluidity and flexibility about the way in which the performers each gain prominence at certain stages of the number without ever dominating, to the extent of making the others subordinate. If anything, there is a mutual trade-off between the performers as they each make way for the others' contributions, often adjusting their own performing styles in response. In

embodying these qualities of versatility and individuality of expression, the performances are crucial to the overall progressive feel of the number, encouraging us, as they do, to feel a sense of joy at the characters' ability to find some release from the more rigidly structured conventions of the all black production.

This notion of gaining release is particularly evident in the case of Petunia who undergoes a marked transition during the course of the number. The sense of change brought about by the music is registered right from the outset as her initial resistance to singing (following Joe's request for her to do so) begins to break down. Having first adopted a rather negative, deferential stance (turning away from Joe and looking bashfully downwards before shaking her head in an almost child-like gesture of refusal) she then assumes a much more confident, open posture as she looks upwards and directly ahead, her face beaming, and begins to sing. The way in which Joe introduces the song ('The one you sang the first time we...' he reminds Petunia who stops him from going any further by calling out his name with a mixture of pleasure and surprise) is also important in highlighting the nature of the release that Petunia undergoes. For by implicitly associating the song with the couple's first kiss, Joe's comment hints at his wish to reawaken a more romantic side to their relationship – and, indeed, to Petunia's character. The transformative effect of the music is further demonstrated during the course of the song itself, the lyrics of which allow Petunia to celebrate her newly rekindled desires in ways that also involve a significant deviation from her religious faith:

Oh, here I go again
I'm hearing trumpets blow again
All aglow again
Taking a chance on love.
Here I slide again
About to take that ride again
Starry eyed again
Taking a chance on love.
I thought the cards were a frame-up
But I never would try
But now I'm taking the game up
And the ace of hearts is high.
Things are mending now
I see a rainbow blending now
We'll have our happy ending now
Taking a chance on love.
Here I slip again
I'm going to take that tip again
Got my grip again

Taking a chance on love.
And now I'll prove again
That I can make life move again
In the groove again
Taking a chance on love.
I'm walking round with a horseshoe
And in clover I lie
Why Mr Rabbit of course you'd better kiss your foot goodbye.
On the ball again
I'm riding for a fall again
I'm gonna give my all again
Taking a chance on love.

Given the references in earlier scenes to the devoutness of Petunia's faith and her expressed commitment to helping Joe renounce his gambling ways and return to the Church, her use of a gambling metaphor to articulate what is a very secular notion of romantic love (one based more upon the forces of chance and good luck rather than upon divine ordination) is highly significant in its implications,[6] suggesting, as it does, an impulse on her part to break free from the restrictions of her role as the 'good Christian black woman' within the narrative. In offering this reading, it should be made clear that it is *the role* of 'good Christian black woman' (that is, as stereotypically defined within white mainstream culture and as used so often in the all-black production) that Petunia (and the film) can be understood as attempting to break free from here more so than actual black Christianity itself, the complexities of which – especially in terms of its music – cannot be defined simply in terms of constraint or as purely in opposition to the likes of jazz.

The need to distinguish between a white stereotypical and more authentic notion of black Christianity is something that we have already come across in our analysis of the earlier *Cabin in the Sky* number where Ethel Waters' improvisatory use of blues notes was able to contest the caricaturing tendencies of the lyrics. Linked to this, one could add that Waters' earlier exuberant rendition of the song 'Li'l Black Sheep' in church near the beginning of the film (when amidst the congregation – consisting of members of the Hall Johnson choir – she stood up and delivered the final rousing refrain) also succeeds in evoking a more celebratory, joyous side to black Christianity that challenges the latter's repressive associations elsewhere in the narrative. In doing so, Waters' performance during this number gestures towards the possibility of a more productive relationship between the black woman and her religion for in playing such a prominent singing role in the church her character is able to achieve a voice and authority outside of the domestic cabin sphere that she otherwise would not have. Taking such performance tendencies into account, then, it is possible to understand the 'Li'l Black Sheep, 'Cabin in the Sky' and 'Taking a Chance on Love' songs as operating more in terms of a continuum than a strict opposition, with the later number providing opportunities for a further release of creative black female impulses that had earlier been channelled into and subordinated to the needs of Petunia's religion.

The opening lyrics of 'Taking a Chance on Love' help manage and reflect this transition in Petunia's character through their initial mixing of secular and religious imagery. The phrase 'I'm hearing trumpets blow again' can, for example, be read both as a jazz band and religious reference (in the American South, the phrase 'hearing trumpets blow' can be understood, in the latter sense, to mean 'On death's door' or 'Skating on thin ice'). Similarly, the line 'Here I *slide* again', although understandable on one level in purely secular terms, also carries with it religious connotations through the associations of the penultimate word with the term 'backsliding' (note also the continuity of the word 'slide' with the earlier idea of 'skating on thin ice'). But if this initial interplay between secular and religious imagery articulates a certain negotiation on Petunia's part between these two sides to her identity (as her desire to give in to her romantic inclinations is expressed in ways that edge it with a sense of religious caution) then overall the rest of the song provides the occasion for a much fuller release of her creative energies. This is evident not just in the lyrics' recurring emphasis on 'Taking a *chance* on love' (the meaning of which contrasts quite noticeably with the equivalent stress in 'Li'l Black Sheep' on the sinner being '*safe* in the fold once more') but also in the much greater scope the number affords for vocal improvisation on Waters' part. The latter tendency manifests itself quite early on in fact through the singer's playful, inventive engagement with the lyrics and her habit of laughing and nodding her head in response to certain lines and is something that becomes much more pronounced in the next section of the number as she proceeds to adjust her singing in response to the jazz-style rhythms of Bill Bailey's tap dancing.

The impact of Bailey's dancing upon Waters' rendition of the song can be accounted for partly in terms of the sheer number and speed of the taps which introduce far more beats to each line of the song than before, and partly by the way that he varies the rhythm of his taps at certain points in the routine. This shifts from medium fast at the beginning to very fast (as he repeatedly taps the toe and then heel of his right foot down on the floor in a rapid feathering movement) to slow (the effect of which is exaggerated by Bailey moving his arms upwards and outwards then back down again in an action reminiscent of a bird flapping its wings). Waters responds by placing more stress upon individual words and parts of a word within each line of the lyrics than before and by stretching out certain lines to accommodate his slowing down of the musical rhythms. Hence, the line 'So I'm taking a whack at any black cat that I see' is delivered using the following distinct points of emphasis (italics indicate where particular words or syllables are stressed while hyphens mark where a pause is inserted between words): 'So I'm taking a *whack at* any *black – cat – that* I *see*' (the 'ee' of this last word is extended considerably). This much freer style of improvisation also involves a creative play with both the shape of the words and the tonal structure of the melody, with the word 'surely' being pronounced as 'shoo-oo-lly' (delivered at the higher end of Waters' vocal range) while 'lost' comes across as 'lawst' (the rounding out of this word is uttered in the tone of a bassier, deeper growl). These tendencies in Waters' voice become even more apparent in the next section of the number when, as Anderson begins to dance, she dispenses with the lyrics altogether and adopts a form of singing that, in its use of scatting ('Dee dar dee dar, dar...') and sliding up and down the musical scales seems much less bound by either the rules of language or the conventional patterns of the melody. It is a form of vocal extemporisation that, drawing on a tradition of improvisation absolutely central to the whole African American aesthetic of music and dance,[7] is crucial in articulating Petunia's desire to deviate from the more stereotypical limitations of her role.

The comical dance routine that Anderson performs during this part of the number signals a corresponding loosening up of Joe's character too as he, like Petunia, enjoys a temporary interlude from work. Yet whereas Bailey's modern style of tap had allowed the younger dancer to overcome the spatial restrictions of the cabin by moving around its interior quite freely, expanding his arms and legs upwards and outwards into space and revolving his whole body at certain points, Anderson's use of an earlier flat-footed style of dancing (consisting of a series of sliding movements across the floor) conveys a sense of his character being much more inhibited by the cabin sphere. The sliding nature of Anderson's footwork is crucial in registering this sense of constraint for not only does it render his dance silent (in contrast to the dynamic sounds of the younger dancer's percussive footwork) but it also conveys the impression of his feet being stuck to the cabin floor (unlike Bailey who is able to project his whole body into the air). Anderson's tendency to move his feet jerkily in opposite directions while turning his head backwards and forwards from one character to another also conveys a sense of uncertainty and a lack of control regarding

the direction of his movements, the effect of which is reinforced by the accompanying looks of surprise that appear on his face as his feet begin to move.

So while the musical and comedic aspects of Anderson's dance routine enable Joe to obtain some form of pleasurable release during the course of the number, they also register a sense of his entrapment and confusion within the narrative world, as a character caught not only between the competing forces of Heaven and Hell but also between the ideologically stereotyped choices of 'good Christian black'/reliable husband on the one hand and backsliding black/deviant male figure on the other. The relevance of gender concerns to Joe's situation is highlighted by the moment where he accidentally burns himself on the kitchen stove. As well as providing another illustration of how hampered he is by the cabin environment, this incident serves to relate the source of his discomfort back to his wife – or, more precisely, to her domestic role and the traditional gender-ordered world that her cooking represents (note, in this context, how Petunia was earlier shown trying to keep Joe's meal warm on the stove while chiding him gently for arriving home 'a little late').

In analysing Anderson's dance routine in ways that interpret his sliding footwork in terms of constraint, one could be accused of imposing

onto this sequence a white Eurocentric, aristocratic view of what it means to be 'into the ground' when in fact in many folk forms (white and black) this kind of dancing is valued as a way of gaining contact with the earth and spirituality (the ring shuffle is one example of this kind of dance). Yet while it is possible that certain cultural assumptions about what 'upward' and 'downward' movements mean may have played a part in the analysis and

while this issue is raised by way of highlighting some of the culturally and racially specific ways in which dance and music can be interpreted, there are black accounts of African American dance that do in fact lend strong support to this reading. In a television documentary on the history of tap, for example, Brenda Dixon Gottschild explains how:

> Tap's origins go back to plantation-era practice where Christianity frowned on dancing and the drum had been outlawed along with African dance. So Africans found ways of making body percussion, foot percussion – using shuffle steps, syncopated steps and found ways of dancing, not in a European or white sense, but without ever lifting or crossing the feet. (Gottschild in *Fascinatin' Rhythm: The Story of Tap* (2001))

According to this kind of account, the development of a close-to-the-floor (and, in some cases, silent) form of black footwork can be understood as emerging in direct response to the experience of slavery, with African Americans adapting their dancing styles in ways that both acknowledged yet also sought to overcome the oppressive effects of white domination. As such, it is a reading that seems quite consistent with the interpretation here of Anderson's dance routine, the significance of which – in conveying a sense of Joe being both temporarily released from and yet still inhibited by the cabin environment – is something that we have arrived at through a detailed attention to the narrative context within which the number occurs.

The sense of tension that is evident within Anderson's performance is mirrored even more extremely in Waters' case through the marked contrast that arises in the next section of the number between her singing (which continues to become increasingly improvisatory in nature) and her danc-

ing which, in its adoption of a rather formal white European rather than flexible African American style of movement,[8] is noticeably far more restrained. This is most evident during the sequence where Anderson places one finger on the top of Waters' head while gesturing with his other hand for her to circle round. The tightly circumscribed nature of her actions here – as she responds by moving round in a slow, ambling kind of way – serves to make clear how, as the domesticated black female responsible for carrying out the various chores in the kitchen, it is her character who is the one most constrained of all by the cabin environment. Thus, while Joe's sliding step movements across the floor limit his body's ability to move *up* into space, at least they enable him to move laterally *around* the cabin at speed and in a range of different directions – in contrast to Petunia whose dancing here barely requires her to move from the spot.

The playful nature of the performances does go some way towards offsetting this sense of restriction as Waters' dainty pointed-toe gestures and

Anderson's mock haughty facial expressions at times seem to transform their routine into a parody of white, upper-class formality. But, overall, the tension in Waters' performance here points to a key conflict in her character, with the voice expressing a proclivity to break free from the kind of racial and gender constraints that her more inhibited, conventional bodily movements serve to reflect. Then, as if unable to sustain this tension any longer, Waters suddenly bursts out into a more uninhibited form of song and dance, the guttural, deep-throated growl she emits at this point being accompanied by a much more vigorous, unrestrained thrusting outwards of her arms and legs. This more extreme casting off of inhibitions is swiftly

stifled, in character terms, by Joe who (countering his earlier request for his wife to sing) calls out Petunia's name in shocked response at her behaviour. In responding to this prohibitive calling out of her character's name by recomposing herself to sing the song's title line once again, Waters still manages (through her re-evocation of the gambling metaphor) to end the number on a subversive note although in doing so she is now required to recontain her recent outburst of energy within the more structured parameters of the lyrics.

In seeking to explore the relevance of this number to the rest of the film, we will concentrate mainly on its importance in opening up a more deviant side to Petunia's character, the implications of which seem absolutely central to an understanding of the progressiveness of *Cabin in the Sky*'s concerns. To understand just how integral this number is to the film's treatment of race and gender, we will now focus upon its relationship to two other key parts of the dream narrative: the earlier encounter that took place between Petunia and two of Joe's gambling associates in the garden of the couple's home and the later sequence that occurs in the nightclub.

On turning first to the scene where Jim Henry (Ernest Whitman) and Dude (Nicodemus) turn up at the garden of the couple's home intent on recovering the gambling debts owed to them by Joe, a striking connection with the 'Taking a Chance on Love' number begins to emerge. For in showing Petunia offering to settle her husband's debts by shooting dice on a 'double or nothing' basis, this sequence provides another instance of where the notion of gambling is used to highlight a more wayward tendency in the Ethel Waters character, her literal engagement here in a game of dice anticipating her later metaphorical appropriation of gambling in song. In this case, though, her recourse to gambling arises not in relation to some spontaneous outburst of musical feeling but as part of a more knowing ploy to expose Joe's gambling associates as cheats. Thus, having twice rolled the dice given to her without success, she proceeds to foil Jim Henry's attempt to switch to another set of dice when it is his turn to play by snatching them from him and rolling them out herself, the much higher score she achieves on this occasion confirming her suspicion that they have been tricking Joe in this manner all along. It is a display of gambling know-how that Petunia tries to justify in religious terms afterwards when, having sent Jim Henry and Dude packing, she stands at the gate and, looking  up at the skies, makes the following apologetic appeal: 'Oh Lord, please forgive me for backsliding. But sometimes when you fight the devil you've got to jab him with his own pitchfork.'

Although Petunia seeks to downplay this aberration in her behaviour by using a religious rationale as the basis for her defence, her actions are in fact much more unorthodox and far-reaching in their implications than what she is prepared to allow for here. By outwitting the gamblers in this way, she displays, to begin with, a worldly-wise resourcefulness and astuteness that belies the more naïve, entrusting religious outlook that she adopts elsewhere, the stereotypical nature of which was shown as having the effect not only of blinding her to the racial hardships of the couple's situation but also of binding her into an unquestioning, cheerful acceptance of the gender servitude that her domestic role involves. The ability of such an outlook to render her oblivious to the oppressiveness of her situation is demonstrated later on at the picnic when, on hearing Joe promise to relieve her toils by buying her an electric washing machine, she is shown exclaiming in disbelief at the extent of her good fortune: 'Little Joe, you're just about to kill me with kindness!' And on actually receiving this gift for her birthday (just before performing the 'Taking a Chance on Love' number), she replies on that occasion with even greater humility: 'Ain't nobody got no right being happy as I am.'

What makes the dice-throwing scene so important in this respect is that it is precisely this persona of the naïve, deferential black woman that Petunia is shown putting on in much more knowing fashion as she sets about duping the gamblers into going along with her plan. 'Well, Jim

Henry, you being such a big-time sport, you wouldn't take advantage of somebody like me who don't know nothing about gambling, would you?' she asks while smiling at him in a manner that seems designed to pander to his assumptions of her as a gullible, rural black woman whose simple faith blinds her to the more corrupt ways of the world. It is a remarkably self-conscious act of performance on her part and one that, in showing her artfully playing out this stereotype for Jim Henry's benefit, serves to make visible the constructed nature of the role that elsewhere she assumes in more transparent, earnest fashion.

The 'Taking a Chance on Love' number's ability to pick up and develop the significance of this other key element of the dice-throwing scene (in addition to reworking the gambling metaphor in the way explored earlier) is highlighted by one detailed, rhyming moment of performance on the part of Waters herself. As she utters with great humility the words 'Ain't nobody got no right being happy as I am' on receiving the gift of the electric washing machine, she can be seen fidgeting with her apron and

looking down meekly in a manner that closely mirrors the repertoire of gestures that she had earlier adopted when asking Jim Henry not to take advantage of her lack of gambling experience (on that occasion she was shown fidgeting with one of the buttons on her calico dress while casting her eyes downwards in a similarly submissive manner). In echoing her earlier gestures in this way, Waters' behaviour here draws attention to an element of perform-

ance in Petunia's relationship with Joe as well, the more self-inhibiting aspects of which are then replaced by a highly creative, affirmative form of musical performance. Indeed, one could summarise the difference between these two otherwise closely related sections of the film by saying that, if the dice-throwing incident manages to expose the more stereotypical aspects of Petunia's role as the 'good Christian black woman', then the musical number develops matters a stage further by gesturing towards the possibility of a more individual, distinctive black female identity emerging once these layers and masks of social performance have been stripped away.

If the 'Taking a Chance on Love' number is able to follow through the implications of the earlier dice-throwing scene in this way, then it also anticipates Petunia's dramatic transformation later on in the film. This occurs when, having sent Joe away from their home (after catching him in an apparently compromising encounter with Georgia Brown (Lena Horne)), she appears at Jim Henry's Paradise club dressed in glamorous clothing (rather than her usual calico dress) and celebrating her newfound sense of freedom by launching into a song that on this occasion requires no prompting  or inducement from her husband. By showing Petunia casting off the stereotypical garb of 'good Christian black woman' and moving out of the remote, folkish world of the cabin into an urban-style space that is so well suited to her earlier gravitation towards gambling and jazz, this later sequence manages to enact, in much more extreme fashion, that overall trajectory of release that took place during the course of the 'Taking a Chance on Love' number. So disruptive to the kind of rigid stereotyping that Bogle associates with the film, this transformation radically extends the two-fold nature of that earlier release, with Petunia's newfound recognition of the oppressiveness of her gender situation and her desire to rebel against it in this case helping to bring about a much more complete rejection of her stoical, religious black persona. The extent of the change that she undergoes is highlighted by the way that, in stark contrast to her earlier cheerful acceptance of her domestic chores and her display of humble gratitude at receiving the gift of an electric washing machine, she now responds to Joe's bemused enquiry – 'Petunia, is this really you?' – with the words: 'Mmhum, but not the same "me" who used to break her back busting suds over a tub for you!'

In a further outright rejection of her former role, she proceeds to celebrate the power of her female sexuality by singing the very song that Georgia Brown had earlier performed on her arrival at the club, thereby also disrupting (in the process) that stereotypical opposition between 'good' and 'bad' black woman that Bogle invokes in his discussion of the film. On completing this song, Petunia then begins to dance in a manner that, now unconstrained by the spatial and ideological confines of the cabin environment, seems to fulfil what had earlier been gestured at by her sudden, hurriedly stifled outburst at the end of the 'Taking a Chance on Love' number. After an initial routine with Domino (a performance that itself constitutes a break away from the kind of emotional dependency upon her husband that she had earlier celebrated in her first rendition of the song 'Happiness

is a Thing Called Joe'), she moves into a more improvised dance sequence of her own, kicking her legs into the air (both in front and to either side of her) and shaking her full body in ways that celebrate her newfound freedom of movement. This ability to expand into space is also emphasised by her act of grabbing her partner's hat at one point and using it as a target for her leg kicks while he struggles unsuccessfully to reach it. And in a gesture of independence that recalls Petunia's earlier tendency to turn away from Joe and project her voice in a different direction at certain points during her rendition of 'Taking a Chance on Love', she dances this section of the number with her back to Domino for much of the time before then advancing towards him while singing an extract from 'Honey in the Honeycomb' again. Domino responds by retreating backwards, the comically defensive nature of his actions playfully expressing his sense of intimidation at this exuberant display of active, independent femininity on her part.

Given the exhilarating nature of Petunia's performance here and the film's overall commitment to freeing her from her former role, the question arises as to why her rebellion should then be shown being closed down so quickly afterwards. As the number ends and the young couples whose dancing had earlier evoked such a sense of freedom crowd onto the dance floor, the environment becomes increasingly claustrophobic for Petunia as she finds herself subject to Domino's unwelcome sexual attentions. Distressed by Domino's behaviour, she calls out to Joe who, on coming to her rescue, gets involved in a fight with his rival. Horrified by what she sees, Petunia responds by lapsing back into her former reliance on divine intervention: 'Lord! Do something about this! Hear my prayer! Take down your wrath and destroy this wicked place!' she cries, at which point a tornado appears and destroys the nightclub but not before she and Joe are both shot 'dead' by Domino.

In one sense, of course, it is possible to see this sequence as reflecting the ideological pressure on the film to conform to the conservative conventions of the all-black musical (not to mention the musical genre as a whole) as Petunia's encounter with Domino helps to trigger a chain of events that results in her reversion to her former role and the couple's reunion and eventual return to the cabin sphere. Yet as the culmination of other important tendencies at work during the build up to this sequence, the incident involving Domino is also indicative of a further insightfulness on the film's part with regard to race and gender. By showing how Petunia's movement into the nightclub sphere eventually renders her vulnerable to another form of gender oppression, the film displays a readiness to combine its progressive investment in releasing the domesticated black female from the restrictions of her former position with a perceptive understanding of the ongoing difficulty of achieving freedom from social stereotyping. This complexity of perspective retrospectively endows her performance of the song 'Honey in the Honeycomb' with another level of significance. Although she clearly sings it in celebration of her newfound sense of emancipation, the irony is that in singing the song that Georgia Brown had performed moments earlier she ultimately ends up becoming prone to the same kind of sexual objectification within the nightclub world as that applied to the Lena Horne character.

That it is Domino who subjects Petunia to this kind of treatment is particularly ironic considering how this character was earlier shown singing about his own tendency to be objectified on account of his physical appearance. This took place prior to the other main characters' arrival when, on being complimented on how 'sharp' he looks by one of the women in the club, Domino proceeds to launch into a performance of the song 'Shine'. Having sung in more general terms about what it is about him that makes him 'feel well-dressed', he then moves on to deliver what is, within the context of the all-black musical form, a surprisingly explicit allusion to white society's tendency to stereotype blacks according to this and other physical traits:

And that is just the reason why
The folks all nickname me – just me.

'Cos my hair is curly
And because my teeth are pearly
And just because I always wear a smile
And suits to dress up in the latest style.
Gee, I'm glad I'm living
Why, I take trouble all with a smile.
Just because my colour's shady
A wee bit different maybe
That's why they call me 'Shine'.

While the words don't go so far as to advocate the singer's resistance to being stereotyped as the smiling black and city dandy, there are certain aspects to Sublett's performance that help to push the song in more defiant directions than the lyrics can manage on their own. When he sings the line 'Cos my hair is curly', for example, he removes his hat and strokes his hair with a delicacy and pride of gesture that contests, rather than merely reinforces, the reductiveness of the stereotype. And as the lyrics disappear altogether at one point, Sublett's dancing (as he skips around the room, cane resting casually on shoulder) and the audience's exuberant clapping combine to transform the number into a quite joyous display of black communal feeling, the progressive effect of which is magnified by the presence of Duke Ellington (that most sophisticated and accomplished of African American composers) in the background. The end of the number is marked by Sublett's assumption of a more self-consciously ironic, almost parodic performance of the high-strutting dandy role when, as the people in the club sing 'That's why they call him "Shine"', he strides up the stairs, exaggerating each of his steps as he reaches the top before tilting his hat and casting a broad-beamed smile at the camera as he exits, in stage-like fashion, from the scene.

By following this number with the sequence showing first Georgia Brown and then Petunia becoming the main focus of attention, as they too arrive at the club glamorously dressed and capable of causing a stir among the crowd of people gathered there, the film constructs the overall scene in ways that seem designed to highlight the parallel ways in which blacks and women are defined in terms of their physical looks and appearance. In Georgia Brown's case, the sequence showing the crowd admiring her clothing and her showing off her 'accessories' invites particularly close comparison with the earlier one involving Domino. However, when it comes to her rendition of 'Honey in the Honeycomb', the lyrics are able to go a stage further than their equivalent in 'Shine' by insisting on the power of the woman's femininity to resist being defined in purely super-ficial terms:

> What have I got
> That the others ain't
> That always seems to please?
> T'ain't my perfume
> Nor my fancy paints.
> But when I charm
> The men all swarm
> Just like they was bees.
> There's honey in the honeycomb
> There's sugar in the cane
> There's oysters in a real oyster stew
> And bubbles in sweet champagne.
> There's jelly in the jelly roll
> And sap in every tree
> Oh there's honey in the honeycomb
> And, honey, there's love in me.

As mentioned earlier, this parallel between Domino and the two women serves to invest the sequence where Sublett's character harasses Petunia with considerable irony. For having just sung about his own proneness to be objectified as a black man he is then shown subjecting Petunia to a gender equivalent of such stereotyping (note, in this respect, how his act of stroking her hair here both echoes and problematises his earlier gesture of stroking his own hair on the line "Cos my hair is curly'). And in a further ironic complication to that overall trajectory of release referred to earlier, Petunia is herself shown becoming implicated in the performance of certain socially-entrapping forms of behaviour during her various verbal exchanges with Joe and Georgia Brown at the club. This is demonstrated most clearly by some of her wise-cracking remarks, the humour of which, while quite pleasurable to the extent of revealing a newfound feistiness and rebelliousness of spirit, tends to work in ways that reinforce the idea of gender and racial stereotyping. On one occasion, for example, she responds to Georgia Brown's assertion: 'I'm speaking my mind' by retorting: 'And I ain't heard a sound', the implication being that she sees her rival in reductively sexist terms as 'all beauty, no brains'. And when being asked by Jim Henry what she would like to drink, Petunia responds (after a quick derisory glance in Joe's direction) with the following implied put-down of her husband's masculinity: 'You may give me a double King Kong.' What makes this latter jibe particularly disturbing is the way that, in seeking to mock Joe's gender status by unfavourably comparing his diminutive stature with the figure of the giant ape alluded to by the name of the drink, she also invokes a white racist notion of black male sexuality as a rampant, threatening force. This problematic aspect to Petunia's humour is also evident in the other jokes she makes at Joe's expense, many of which, in seeking to reinforce her claim to an equal share of the sweepstake money, have the effect of locking him even more oppressively back into his financial role:

Joe:	Why, you're, you're beautiful, Petunia.
Petunia:	Oh, save that sugar-coated talk for your girlfriend.
Joe:	Where did you get the clothes?
Petunia:	Don't you worry about that, pops. The main point is, you're paying for 'em.
Joe:	Course. Course I'll pay for 'em. I didn't realise.
Petunia:	And that ain't all I'm collecting before I'm through.
Joe:	Oh, don't talk like that Petunia. You know I still love you.

Then, a bit later on...

Petunia:	I'm sending my lawyer round to see you and he'd better find you in.
Joe:	What for?
Petunia:	Money, what you think?! And if you ain't saved my half, brother, start sprouting wings.
Joe:	But what's wings?
Petunia:	That's one way of getting out of jail. I know all about that sweep stake money and I'm solid collecting my

	half, cash on the line.
Joe:	But, I don't know if I've got that much left, Petunia.
Petunia:	No? Then you're just in the correct suit to be laid out in.

In the last of an intricate series of parallels, the film proceeds to highlight the allied pressures inherent in Joe and Petunia's new situations as they

are each shown becoming caught up in an increasingly stifling relationship with their alternative partner figures. This is dramatised most vividly during the closed couple-dancing sequence when, in an echoing series of images, the film cuts back and forth from a shot showing Domino harassing Petunia (as she grows uneasy at his unwelcome attentions and struggles to get free) to one showing Georgia Brown clinging onto Joe (as he tries to pull away from her). By presenting us with this rhyming pair of images, the film draws attention to the mutually oppressive nature of such gender roles for men and women, with Joe becoming ensnared by Georgia Brown on account of his perceived worth financially and Petunia being harassed by Domino on account of her assumed easy availability in sexual terms.

If Petunia's retreat into her former ways can therefore be understood partly as a response on her part to the growing oppressiveness of the nightclub sphere, then when viewed with-in the context of the dream framework, the incident involving her and Domino can also be read, in more subjectively male terms, as an attempt by the dreamer Joe to censor or deny his previously expressed wish to release his wife from the burdens of her domestic position. The desire for this, having earlier found safer outlet during the 'Taking a Chance On Love' number, is now enacted (from his perspective) in more threatening, anxiety-ridden terms through her rebellious appearance at the club. By prompting a scenario whereby Joe then has to come to Petunia's rescue on the dance floor, the dream consequently allows him to recontain her within a more traditionally passive gender role while at the same time enabling him to prove his masculinity through an act of heroic devotion towards his wife (note, too, how Joe's actual shooting by Domino near the beginning of the film is reconstrued here in ways that cast Anderson's character in a much more favourable, courageous light).

On another level, these censoring aspects to Joe's dream are also symptomatic of what was referred to earlier as the film's own ideological obligation to recontain *its* more subversive impulses within the conservative framework of the all-black musical. Yet while *Cabin in the Sky* does ostensibly comply with such pressures, the precise manner in which it handles Petunia's reversion to her former faith has the effect of imbuing this retreat into a more folkish world view with a great deal of irony.

Particularly notable in this regard is its borrowing of the tornado imagery from *The Wizard of Oz* (Victor Fleming, 1939) for the divine retribution sequence (see Minnelli 1974: 126). By employing the special effects that were originally used to transport Dorothy and her house away from Kansas to the mythical land of Oz, the film enables us to read the tornado here not as an act of divine intervention brought on by the power of Petunia's faith but as a kind

of ironic *deus ex machina* or fantasy device produced entirely through the illusion-making medium of cinema. And when Petunia (now supposedly a ghost) once again resorts to prayer in the ensuing judgement scene, her plea for divine clemency and understanding results in the appearance of a large staircase that seems, in its elaborate design, to originate less from heaven and more, as James Naremore observes, 'from a Ziegfeld production number' (1993: 66). The fact that Joe's dream begins to break down at the very point when he and Petunia ascend the stairs to heaven also tends to problematise Bogle's claim that, 'in the end, Petunia's prayers save him [Joe], and together the two are able to walk to their cabin in the sky' (1994: 129). By closing this sequence down before the couple actually arrive in heaven and just as Joe can be heard anxiously asking 'Do you think I can make it? ... Can I make it? ... Do you think I can make it?' the film instead seems to hint both at his unconscious resistance to fulfilling this supposed goal of his dream and at its own lack of conviction in the attainability of this ideal.

Arguably, though, it is the musical numbers themselves that provide the most powerful, lasting resistance to this ideological recontainment of Petunia by the end of the dream. The sense of release and empowerment conveyed by her dance in the nightclub endows her transformation with an intensity and force of feeling that challenges the kind of token explanation of her behaviour that is offered later on in the judgement scene when the General (Kenneth Spencer), having 'balanced the books', agrees to overlook what he refers to as 'this little setback tonight' on the basis that she was 'just acting up to get Little Joe back again'. And while a narrative-based reading of the film might construe Petunia's rebellion as an act motivated solely by her mistaken assumption (on seeing Joe with Georgia Brown in the garden of their home) that he is double-crossing her, her performance during the 'Taking a Chance on Love' number crucially insists on the possibility of a more transgressive side to her character long before her break-up with Joe. Indeed, rather than viewing Petunia's angry outburst at Joe, on seeing him with Georgia Brown, as the cause of her rebellion in the nightclub it is possible to see this moment as itself constituting a darker narrative embodiment of what was first released in more joyful, unthreatening form in that earlier number. This is suggested by the precise way in which the General reprimands Petunia for sending Joe away: 'Petunia, *you didn't even give him a chance*', his negative inversion of the song's title line encouraging us to read her outburst here both as a re-suppression of the more positive feelings for Joe that had emerged in that earlier number and as a more desperate manifestation of her growing frustration and desire to break free from the constraints of her position.

The fact that Petunia celebrates Joe's recovery from his dream by singing 'Taking a Chance on Love' to him once again provides yet further proof of the music's importance in resisting this recontainment of the Ethel Waters character at the end. By allowing Petunia to sing the song that had earlier signalled, in such pleasurable fashion, the emergence of a more deviant side to her character, the film re-evokes these impulses in a way that gives them an independent life and ongoing validity outside of the dream, thereby resisting, in turn, the more conservative implications arising from the couple's return to the cabin sphere. In doing so, the film invites us to take something much more enjoyably subversive from the dream than Joe who, terrified by the fact that he 'almost didn't get into heaven', interprets his 'narrow escape' as a vindication of Petunia's religious faith. The contrast between Joe and Petunia's reactions to the dream could not be more different in fact. For if Joe's instruction to Petunia to burn his sweepstake ticket and calamity cubes signals his cowed submission to the Church, then this is countered by the Ethel Waters character's

reappropriation of the gambling metaphor in song, having dismissed his attempts to explain the religious import of his dream with the words: 'Oh well. Let's not talk about that now. Let's talk about how happy you've made me now that you've come back.' In reopening the narrative – and the couple's relationship – to these more progressive tendencies, *Cabin in the Sky* ends by suggesting that, in contrast to the ostensible ideal embodied in its title, it is in the more liberating possibilities of the 'Taking a Chance on Love' number that the film's utopian sensibility more convincingly lies.

Studies of racial and gender oppression in West Side Story and Fiddler on the Roof

As two further examples of musicals that seek to offer a progressive treatment of race and gender, *West Side Story* (Robert Wise, 1961) and *Fiddler on the Roof* (Norman Jewison, 1971) are both interesting for the way that they combine an analysis of racist hostilities *between* cultures with a study of the patriarchal oppression of women *within* the individual cultures themselves. *West Side Story*'s opening dance sequence depicting the movement of the white gang, the Jets, through the urban slums of New York as they seek to assert their territorial supremacy over the rival Puerto Rican gang, the Sharks, is particularly fascinating to consider in relation to Dyer's article 'The Colour of Entertainment'. What it offers, in effect, is a notable instance of where a major MGM musical self-consciously dramatises the processes by which the whiteness of the urban spaces of America are both asserted and contested through the expansionist movements of the white and Hispanic male dancers as they each make their way through the streets of Manhattan. It is a struggle for territorial control that, as the exclusion of the women from these and other staged moments of rivalry indicates, perhaps reveals as much about the shared masculinist ideals underpinning the two groups as about the racial antagonisms operating between them. One qualification to this can be found in the balletic nature of the male dancers' movements, the expressive qualities of which, while in one sense serving to convey the rival gang members' attempts to reach out and claim control of the spaces around them, also hints at a more creative, non-aggressive potential to their characters.

In depicting the women's resistance to the patriarchal structures of control operating within their respective cultures (mainly via an emphasis on the white rebel female's attempts to gain acceptance by the Jets and the efforts by Anita (Rita Moreno) to challenge her boyfriend Bernardo's (George Chakiris) sexist expectations), *West Side Story* invites particularly strong comparison with *Fiddler on the Roof*. In the case of this later film, though, its account of three Jewish daughters' struggle to assert their right to marry outside of the conventional arranged marriage structure is complicated by an accompanying exploration of the oppressiveness of such a tradition for the father himself, as Tevye (Topol) is shown becoming increasingly burdened by his duty of upholding this custom in the face of his daughters' emotional pleas to marry the men of their choice. In this sense, *Fiddler on the Roof* also offers an interesting development on Hollywood's first musical, *The Jazz Singer*. While both of these films focus on a story of inter-generational conflict within a traditional Jewish family, *Fiddler on the Roof* is notable for the much greater emphasis that it places on the inner conflict experienced by the Jewish patriarch figure as he struggles (in ways that seem deeply bound up with concerns about the oppressiveness of his own arranged marriage) to reconcile his allegiance to the traditions of his faith with his paternal feelings of love for his daughters.

This more complex treatment of the Jewish patriarch is reflected in the use of the music which, rather than simply serving, as in *The Jazz Singer*, to reinforce the father's obdurate refusal to adapt to the new ways of his adopted country, instead functions as a way of thinking through the inner struggle that is going on within him. Consequently, on those occasions where Tzeitel (Rosalind Harris) and Hodel (Michele Marsh) confront Tevye with their wish to marry a poor tailor and a political revolutionary respectively, his musical response swings from a strident reassertion of the song

'Tradition' to the adoption of a much softer, more lyrical form of singing, one that (occurring in a subjective realm outside of the normal framework of time and space) enables him to respond quite directly to the emotional force of his daughters' feelings: 'But look at my daughter's eyes. She loves him!' The music's potential to bring about some form of release from his more rigid, ingrained ways of thinking breaks down, though, on the third occasion when he receives news that his next oldest daughter, Chava, has secretly married a gentile. Having first engaged in a tender song recalling his memories of his 'little Chaveleh' during the 'Chava ballet' sequence, Tevye's attempt to rationalise his reaction ends with him abruptly terminating such reflections with a loudly prohibitive response to his daughter ('No, Chava, no!') that echoes his predecessor Cantor Rabinowitz's equally vehement reaction (conveyed silently, on that occasion, via intertitle) to hearing his son singing the music of American popular song ('Stop!'). It is a retreat into his traditional way of thinking that (inviting some comparison, too, with Petunia's reversion to her religious faith near the end of the nightclub sequence in *Cabin in the Sky*) drives the Jewish father (like Cantor Rabinowitz before him) into a repressive state of silence as he refuses to acknowledge his daughter's place within the family.

This complex perspective on oppression – as something both external and internal to the Jewish community – culminates in the final section of the narrative when, as Tevye, his wife and younger daughters prepare to leave the village of Anatevka following the edict to this effect, the film counterpoints the eviction of the Jews by the Tsarist government with Tevye's silent expulsion of Chava from the family. Such a parallel is wryly alluded to by Chava's husband Fyedka (Raymond Lovelock) whose bleak assessment of the situation – 'Some are driven away by edicts, others by silence' – is only mollified by the father's last-minute calling out to his daughter as she begins to walk away: 'And God be with you!' The closing sequence showing Tevye (rather than his horse) pulling the cart containing the family's possessions along the road while his wife and children walk alongside vividly dramatises the weight of the material and ideological burden that he is required to shoulder, the one perhaps more hopeful gesture coming in the form of his nod for the fiddler – and the musical spirit of survival he represents – to follow behind.

Both of the above films warrant much fuller analysis than can be given to them here but, along with *Cabin in the Sky* and the two versions of *Show*

Boat studied earlier, they constitute key moments in the genre's history, moments where the musical begins to engage with some of the racial and gender issues that are at stake in the construction of its utopian dreams.

2   WHEN THE WOMAN SINGS: VOICE, IMAGE, IDENTITY

Having examined the crucial role played by the black female singer's voice in *Cabin in the Sky*, let us move on to explore the centrality of the woman's voice to the Hollywood musical more broadly, using the genre's own intense, self-conscious preoccupation with this area as the main focal point of this study. As we shall see, this is a preoccupation that tends to manifest itself in two main ways – on the one hand, taking the form of a fascination (in two key musicals) with the figure of a woman who (usually of lower-class origins) is considered to possess an uncouth, socially unacceptable speaking voice; on the other, finding quite different and much more pervasive expression in a number of backstage musicals dealing with the phenomenon of the great female singer.

Although we will be analysing examples from both of these strands, it is the second category of musical about the great female singer that will form the main focus of study in this chapter. Central to our exploration here will be the possibility of the strong female singer's voice posing some form of disruption or challenge to the traditional gender power structures operating within the narrative worlds, the presence of which often takes the specific form of an influential male director, producer or performer figure who seeks to take control of the woman's performing career and identity. To what extent, for example, does the powerful but intangible nature of the great female singer's voice make her more resistant, more of a threat to male control than, say, the female dancer whose body can often become subject to a range of pressures and constraints within the usually far from glamorous world of the backstage musical? In films like *42nd*

Street (Lloyd Bacon, 1933), such pressures find their most extreme manifestation in the form of the gruelling rehearsal routine (during which the female dancer's body is pushed to the limits of physical endurance by a tyrannical producer or director figure) and in the requirement, particularly acute within the poverty-stricken environment of 1930s Depression-era America, for the female dancer to sell her body in exchange for a part in the show (on *42nd Street*'s 'matter-of-fact acknowledgement of backstage prostitution', see Hoberman 1993: 39).

According to Lucy Fischer, this control of the female dancer's body often extended, in the numbers choreographed by Busby Berkeley for the Warner Bros. backstage musicals of the 1930s, to a textual manipulation of the woman's body as filmic image. Analysing the role played by Berkeley's camerawork and *mise-en-scène* in *Dames* (Ray Enright, 1934), she cites the choreographer's trademark use of overhead shots as one example of how the female chorines are depersonalised and objectified through a process of visual patterning that involves 'their identities [being] completely consumed in the creation of an overall abstract design' (1981: 75):

> This reduction of the female form to biotic tile in an abstract mosaic is not devoid of overtones of power. It tends, in fact, to literalise the stereotype of the male director as potent Svengali who transforms the dull but malleable female form into an alluring screen presence. (Ibid.)

While one can share Bruce Babington and Peter Evans' reservations about the possible over-simplifications that can arise from an exclusive concentration on the sexist aspects of Berkeley's choreography (for a discussion of other more critical tendencies at work in both the numbers and narratives of Warner Bros. musicals, see Babington & Evans 1985: 53), Fischer's detailed account of how the female performer's body is manipulated and controlled in certain numbers does help to throw into extreme relief the potential of the female voice to resist being pinned down in this manner.

Subverting the idea of woman as spectacle in Funny Girl

By way of demonstrating the disruptive impact that the charismatic female singer may have on such traditional objectifications of the female form, let us begin by considering an example from *Funny Girl* (William Wyler, 1968). The sequence in question occurs at that point in the film where the Jewish singer and comedienne Fanny Brice (played by Barbra Streisand), having previously struggled to overcome the perception that she is not beautiful enough (or, in ethnic terms, not Gentile enough) to succeed as a performer on the stage, is given the chance to appear in the Ziegfeld Follies. A major influence on the style of musical spectacle that Busby Berkeley pioneered in the Hollywood musical, the Follies was a long-running and highly successful form of Broadway musical theatre that, produced by the legendary theatrical impresario Florenz Ziegfeld (played in the film by Walter Pidgeon), was noted for its decorative use of glamorous women as the main attraction of the show. Revelling in the disturbance that Streisand poses to this form of musical spectacle, the film shows her character first objecting, during her audition, to Ziegfeld's decision to include her in a number dedicated to extolling the virtues of the beautiful bride and then responding, when he insists that she does appear, with a hilariously improvised performance that undermines his intentions for the show. Introduced by the other female performers as the ultimate paragon of bridal virtue, Streisand's character duly makes her grand entrance on stage dressed in

a wedding gown and flanked on either side by a host of glamorous women, only to then turn sideways to reveal the outline of a heavily pregnant bride.

It is an anarchic moment of improvisation (she confesses later on to having impulsively hidden a cushion underneath her wedding gown just before going on stage) that completely disrupts the conventional flow of the Ziegfeld number, brilliantly undermining, as it does, the latter's somewhat contradictory investment in the image of the virtuous, virginal bride on the one hand and the figure of the glamourised, highly eroticised female body on the other. Perhaps even more importantly in this context, this subversive manipulation of the female image is something that is both initiated and sustained by the charismatic power of the female singer's voice. It was, after all, Ziegfeld's need for 'a strong voice' in the finale that led to Fanny appearing in this number in the first place, the tensions created by the inclusion of such a singing talent within an otherwise very conventional production number thereby serving as the catalyst for the disruptions that follow. And it is Streisand's comic vocal improvisations during the number itself that manage to prolong and develop the female performer's active intervention in this male-constructed spectacle. Her play with the shape and tonal texture of the words is particularly effective in enabling her character to subvert Ziegfeld's earlier instruction ('You will sing the words exactly as written') by generating meanings and inferences only available through the act of performance itself. This is evident in the very opening section of the song when her ironic, questioning style of delivery has the effect of both parodying and transforming the more conventional ideological meanings implicit in the line: 'I am the beautiful reflection of my love's affection', the changed vocal inflection she adopts for the second half of this line being accompanied and reinforced by a quizzical glancing down at the bump on her belly.

One could, of course, argue that the more radical force of this 'pregnant bride' routine is partly qualified by the fact that it is Fanny's apparent lack of confidence in her own looks that prevents her from delivering the song straight. This was made clear during the preceding rehearsal scene when she was shown explaining her reluctance to appear in the finale on the grounds that she is not beautiful enough to sing the lyrics of the song with sufficient conviction. Her explanation to Ziegfeld that 'If I come out opening night telling the audience how beautiful I am, I'll be back at Keeney's before the curtain comes down' amounted, in that instance, to a much more modest denigration of her own image rather than the ideals of femininity embodied in the show. Such a touching display of insecurity derives much of its poignancy from the Jewishness of both Streisand and the character she plays, the self-deprecating nature of the comments suggesting much, in this context, about the female performer's own susceptibility to internalising society's assumptions about what constitute the expected norms and ideals of female beauty.

Yet while Fanny seeks to articulate her reluctance to sing in ways that imply a certain deference to such ethnically prejudiced ways of thinking, Streisand's actual performance during the number itself is far more complex in the way that it mixes moments of self-parody with a more assertive, anarchic style of delivery.[1] This is established during her initial show-stopping appearance on stage when her act of turning sideways to reveal the bump on her belly is executed with a confidence and panache that belies

her character's claims to inadequacy and in a way that also seems to provide the opportunity for a proud, defiant display of the famous Streisand
nose. In flaunting her ethnic difference from the other female performers
in this way, Streisand manages to further the kind of critique of WASP-
ish ideals of femininity that was first put forward by Fanny's mother (Kay
Medford) earlier on in the film. This occurred during the number 'If a Girl
Isn't Pretty' when, on hearing one of her neighbours claim that her daughter is not beautiful enough to succeed on stage, Fanny's mother sought fit
to protest in the following indignant terms: 'Is a nose with deviation such
a crime against the nation?'

The complexity of Streisand's performance during the bridal number
is also encapsulated in her singing of the words: 'I am so beautiful.' While
her croaking delivery of this line seems designed to convey her character's
sense of inferiority at being unable to live up to the idealised images of
womanhood that surround her here, it is a putting down of the character's
looks that, rather tellingly, can only be achieved by the singer disguising
and distorting the natural beauty of her own *voice*. And if Streisand's singing at times becomes marked by this quality of self-deprecation, overall
her anarchically comedic and distinctively Jewish style of vocal delivery is
able to convey the sense of an independent performing self that is much
less deferentially tied to stereotypical notions of female beauty. Ranging
from a mock opera-style ascension of the scales at one point to the
adoption of duck-like quacking sounds at another, her voice displays an
agility and elasticity of form that refuses either to restrict itself to any one
conventional mode of musical delivery or to conform (at least in any deferential sense) to the standard melodic qualities expected from the female
singing voice. As a singing style that 'is marked not just by emotional
mobility, but by something like an actual multiplicity of voices' (Babington
& Evans 1985: 216), it seems particularly resistant to the forms of manipulation and control traditionally practised on the female image in this kind
of number. What it manages to convey is a complex, fluid sense of identity
quite different from the more reductive categorisations of women offered
earlier on in the song.

The ability of Streisand's voice to dislodge the kind of traditional structures of male looking and control associated with this tradition of musical
spectacle is also made clear by the way that her vocal protests consistently
succeed in undermining Ziegfeld's position as a kind of supreme male

voyeur of the show. This began in the previous audition scene when her irreverent calling out to Ziegfeld, as he sits in the balcony of a darkened auditorium waiting for her to perform the song, and her audacious questioning of his decision to put her in the bridal number ('So no one's supposed to argue with the landlord?' she asks on being reminded by him that she is in his theatre) eventually prompts this autocratic producer figure to relinquish his privileged spectator position ('Up above – like God', as one of the other female members of the cast puts it) and come back down to the stage to address her face to face. Such a scenario is re-enacted in more dramatic fashion on opening night when her performance in the bridal number once again gets him up out of his seat high up in the auditorium and sends him down to a position near to the front stalls where he then waits, with glowering but ineffectual stares, for her performance to end. In foregrounding these reactions in the Walter Pidgeon character, the film registers something of the threat that Streisand's voice poses not just to the producer's control over this particular number but to that broader musical tradition of using the woman as object of spectacle that Ziegfeld represents.

Having explored how the disruptive potential of the female singing voice may operate in the precise context of a particular number, let us investigate some of the broader impacts that this sort of voice may have in the Hollywood musical. Using a number of key films, we shall pay particular attention to the kinds of male responses that are provoked by such a voice. To what extent, for example, does the charismatic strength of the woman's singing voice manage to effect some form of genuine recognition, or even transformation, in her influential male mentor figure or does the potency and autonomy of her voice ultimately result in the adoption of even more extreme or elaborate strategies of control? However, before exploring how such matters find expression in a group of backstage musicals dealing with the phenomenon of the great female singer, let us first examine how this potential for disruption finds rather different inflection in a pair of well-known musicals centred on the figure of a woman in possession of an uncouth speaking voice.

The disruptiveness of the female speaking voice in My Fair Lady

Of the two musicals that deal with this – namely, *My Fair Lady* (George Cukor, 1964) and *Singin' in the Rain* – the first is by far the most thoughtful in its sensitivity to the issues at stake. This tendency can be attributed not just to the contributions of Hollywood director George Cukor and the musical song-writing team of lyricist Alan Jay Lerner (who also wrote the screenplay) and composer Frederick Loewe but to the film's origins in Bernard Shaw's play *Pygmalion*. Written in 1912 around the time of the Suffragist movement and displaying evidence of this dramatist's commitment to the rights of women, Shaw's play was itself a critical reworking of the classical Greek myth about the sculptor Pygmalion. As recounted so memorably in Ovid's *Metamorphoses*, this myth dealt with the story of how Pygmalion, on becoming disillusioned with the women of his village, creates the statue of a beautiful woman and, falling in love with his creation, has his prayers answered when Venus (the goddess of love) brings the statue (named Galatea) to life. Relocating the myth of Pygmalion within an early nineteenth-century London setting, Shaw's play about the attempt by Henry Higgins, a professor of phonetics, to transform Eliza Doolittle, a Covent Garden flower girl, into a 'lady' by teaching her to speak 'properly' not only placed more emphasis upon the woman's point of view but also shifted attention onto the man's attempt to create his ideal female through a moulding of the *voice*, primarily, rather than just the image.

In reconstruing the myth in terms of this scenario whereby a professor uses his speech-training expertise to transform a younger, uncultured female into a sophisticated socialite, Shaw's play also reflected the dramatist's interest in phonetics. Underpinning this interest was Shaw's belief that speech and dialect are important determinants of social class and that by learning how to speak 'correctly' a person could improve her/his station in life. Such a belief is articulated by Higgins himself early in the play when, on hearing Eliza speak for the first time in her Cockney dialect, he remarks to Colonel Pickering:

> You see this creature with her kerbstone English: the English that will keep her in the gutter to the end of her days. Well, sir, in three months I could pass that girl off as a duchess at an ambassador's garden party. I could even get her a place as lady's maid or shop assistant, which requires better English.

But this account of a man who exerts a controlling, shaping influence over a young woman's voice also needs to be considered in the context of society's fascination at that time with the Svengali/Trilby relationship, the story of which, hugely popular on its release, had, by the time that Shaw's play was written, become part of the cultural landscape of that era. First published in 1894 and itself the subject of a highly successful stage adaptation as well as two film adaptations, George Du Maurier's novel *Trilby* dealt with the story of Svengali, a professor of music, who uses his special powers of hypnosis to mesmerise a young female model, Trilby, into leaving her lover and, in her new married role as Madame Svengali, embarking on a career as a concert singer in Europe. As another modern, but much darker, reworking of the myth of Pygmalion, Du Maurier's story about a man who uses his hypnotic powers to refashion a young woman's singing voice into that of an accomplished concert singer provides a further important cultural backdrop to Shaw's play.

If these influences contribute considerably to the complexity and thought-provoking nature of the play's subject matter, then they also help to account for a certain tension or contradiction in the text concerning its attitude towards Higgins' transformation of Eliza that *My Fair Lady* tends to reproduce and compound. On the one hand, the film's commitment to offering a musical adaptation of Shaw's reworking of the Pygmalion myth leads it to adopt a quite critical view of Higgins (Rex Harrison) whose insensitive treatment of Eliza (Audrey Hepburn) as the object of a bet blinds him to her deeper feelings. Like the play, therefore, the film contains several moments where various other characters (the housekeeper Mrs Pearce (Mona Washbourne), Colonel Pickering (Wilfred Hyde-White) and Higgins' mother (Gladys Cooper)) protest vehemently about Higgins' treatment of Eliza. And like Shaw's play, the film invites certain gender parallels to be drawn between Higgins and Eliza's father Alfred Doolittle (Stanley Holloway), both of whom are linked, despite the gulf that exists between them in class terms, by their respective verbal and physical cruelty towards Eliza. At times, the film also uses its musical elements to accentuate and develop this aspect of the play's critique. During the phase dealing with Higgins' relentless coaching of Eliza, for example, the song 'Just You Wait 'Enry 'Iggins' is used to enact a fantasy of rebellion on the female protagonist's part and in a manner that allows her Cockney voice to give vent to her desire to gain revenge on her tyrannical tutor. And during the speech-training sequences themselves, the *mise-en-scène* tends to provide yet further confirmation of the brutality of Higgins' regime. In one particularly telling shot that has the effect of construing his speech-training room as a kind of torture chamber, Eliza is shown agonisingly practising her vowels as she sits strapped into a chair while surrounding her on all sides are various intimidating pieces of phonetics 'surveillance' equipment that monitor and record her every vocal inflection.

Yet while these various musical and visual strategies combine to suggest a quite critical view of language as an instrument of male control, elsewhere the film counters this by endorsing Shaw's more optimistic belief in speech training as a means to social improvement and class mobility. This notion, first articulated musically in the form of Higgins' opening song 'Why Can't the English?', finds its ultimate expression during the 'Rain in Spain' number where the utopian aspects of song and dance are used to celebrate the moment where Eliza first discovers how to pronounce her vowels properly. The film emphasises the liberating effects of this newly acquired mode of speech by also using the number to bring about the release of Eliza's romantic desire for Higgins, the actual expression of which (in the follow-on song 'I Could Have Danced All Night') is in turn made possible by her access to this more articulate form of language. But while the joyful singing and dancing of Eliza, Higgins and Colonel Pickering during the 'Rain in Spain' number are very much in tune with this celebratory view of language, the musical reiteration of Eliza's earlier elocution lesson in the lyrics tends to qualify the utopian aspects of the song by foregrounding a notion of language that is still based on the need for hierarchy, regulation and control. 'Now once again, where does it rain?' asks Higgins in a more playful reprisal of his earlier role. 'On the plain! On the plain!' replies Eliza obediently. 'And where's that soggy plain?' pursues Higgins. 'In Spain! In Spain!' In a manner that seems characteristic of the film as a whole, then, it is possible to detect a certain tension or conflict at work within this number. For if the more spontaneous, improvised aspects of the characters' singing and dancing manage to convey a sense of hope about Eliza's ability to gain release from the restrictiveness of her former social position, then what the lyrics themselves would seem to imply, through their overall structure and content, is that any such escape from the strictures of lower-class life can only be achieved through an adherence to the rules and conventions of a dominantly upper-class, male-controlled mode of speech.

In facilitating Eliza's metamorphosis into a beautiful 'princess' or 'lady'-like figure, this vocal transformation also prompts a more conventional reworking of the woman's image than that which occurred during the bridal number in *Funny Girl*. The moment where Eliza appears, elegantly descending the stairs of Higgins' house while glamorously dressed for the embassy ball, poses none of that disruption to male-idealised ways of looking at the female form that Streisand's character managed to achieve through her improvised appearance as a pregnant bride. Audrey Hepburn's performance in the role does endow Eliza's metamorphosis with another level of significance, however. For in undergoing such a transformation in *My Fair Lady*, this female star not only re-enacts a process already well established in films like *Sabrina* (Billy Wilder, 1954) but she also emerges with an image that is much more consistent with her earlier formative roles as elegant princess and chic socialite figure in *Roman Holiday* (William Wyler, 1953) and *Breakfast at Tiffany's* (Blake Edwards, 1961) respectively. The fact that this transformation and the resulting image that Eliza acquires are both such important aspects of Hepburn's star persona could, of course, be seen as undermining our resistance to Higgins' attempts to change her yet further for in bringing about this metamorphosis, he is in a sense helping us to fulfil this key viewing expectation. Yet the fact that Eliza's transformation demands to be read so strongly in terms of Hepburn's star persona makes her metamorphosis much more than simply a product of Higgins' authorship and control.

Indeed, when Eliza emerges with a more sophisticated voice and image in the second half of the film (having discarded the Cockney accent that had earlier seemed so uncomfortable to the female star herself), there is a compelling sense in which it is Hepburn's star identity, rather than simply Higgins' reconstructed version of the female protagonist, that is asserting itself here. Such a reading of this moment is very much in line with the analysis of Rachel Moseley who, while also stressing both the extreme difficulties associated with Eliza's transformation and the fact that 'the results of this enforced labour are more conventionally feminine than in any of her [Hepburn's] other film roles', goes on to argue that:

> Throughout the film ... Eliza gradually becomes more 'like Audrey' in appearance and demeanour, and when she descends the staircase dressed for the embassy ball in the most minimal outfit of the film, an elegant white gown of long, clean lines and simple coif-

fure, the modulation of her voice as she says '*Thank* you, Colonel Pickering' clearly reveals her as 'Audrey Hepburn'. (2002: 73)

(See Moseley, too, for an analysis of the ways in which Hepburn's transformation in this and other films may speak to female audiences' own experiences of growing up and moving upwards in social class terms.)

If this assertion of a more recognisable, more articulate version of Hepburn's star identity helps contribute to the development of a stronger critique of Higgins in the second, post-transformation phase of the narrative, then there are also certain musical numbers that are crucial in enabling the film to extend and deepen its critical reworking of the Pygmalion myth. The 'You Did It' number which takes place immediately after Eliza's successful appearance at the Embassy Ball offers one such example. By contrasting Higgins and Pickering's self-centred celebration of Higgins' moment of triumph with Eliza's sense of exclusion at this point (as she stands silently and largely unnoticed in the background, her contribution to the night's proceedings going completely unacknowledged by the two men), the number succeeds in drawing attention to the male egocentrism underpinning Higgins' enterprise and, by extension, the Pygmalion myth itself. As well as qualifying the celebratory tone of this particular scene, this foregrounding of Eliza's non-participation in the song also has the effect of further problematising the utopian optimism of the earlier 'Rain in Spain' number. The use on this later occasion of such an exclusively male self-congratulatory mode of address serves to expose and bring out much more explicitly the patriarchally controlled nature of the language that she has been taught.

This strategy of excluding Eliza from a musical number so as to highlight the costs and consequences of this transformation for the woman herself is reworked later on during the sequence where she revisits her former haunt at Covent Garden market only to discover that no one recognises her there either. In that instance, Eliza's non-participation in the market traders' reprisal of the song 'Wouldn't it be Loverly?' invites ironic contrast with her earlier ebullient performance of the same number. In registering this shift from central participant to outside observer, the film signals the extent to which her acquisition of the material comforts yearned for in the song's lyrics have been acquired at the cost of a loss of her working-class identity and sense of communal belonging. Eliza's lack of a role in both of these songs thus poignantly reinforces the sense of cultural displacement and disorientation that she expressed so vocally during her outburst against Higgins after the first of these numbers: 'Where am I to go? What am I to do? What is to become of me?' she demanded of him then. In line with Shaw's play, the film seeks to resolve both her confusion and its own inner tension (that is, between a belief in language as a means to achieving social advancement and a critique of language as a controlling male discourse) by allowing Eliza to discover the liberating capacity of speech but in a way that enables her to articulate her right to claim independence from the male who taught her.

Eliza's forceful delivery of the song 'Without You' (performed during the scene where she encounters Higgins at his mother's house following her departure from his place the night before) is the culmination of this. Acting as a generic extension of Eliza's two previous speeches (namely, the one the night before when she railed against Higgins for his insensitivity towards her, and the one just before this number when she compared him unfavourably to Colonel Pickering), this song uses the more liberating, expressive potential of music to lend further conviction to the female protagonist's bid for independence. The defiant declaration of this is evident both in the forward-pushing, upward-thrusting structure of the melody and in the assertiveness of the lyrics themselves:

I shall not feel alone without you.
I can stand on my own without you.
So go back in your shell,
I can do bloody well, without [you]!

Eliza's use of a swearword here, together with Cockney colloquialisms like 'ducky' elsewhere in the lyrics, also contributes to the effectiveness of the song for it suggests how she is now able to combine her newfound sense of independence with those working-class aspects of her identity that she had earlier been forced to suppress. And it is this display of vocal independence that, in prompting Higgins to change his way of viewing Eliza, in turn triggers an important development in the male protagonist himself, the effect of which is again conveyed musically via the final two numbers that Rex Harrison sings.

The first song, 'I Did It' (a reworking of the earlier number 'You Did It'), is a transitional number in this sense. On the one hand expressing

Higgins' admiration for this more independent version of Eliza, it none-theless does so in a way that (through such self-satisfied claims as: 'By George, I really did it! I did it! I did it! I said I'd make a woman and indeed I did!'), makes clear his need to reassert his authorship of this newly trans-formed female. This desire to re-impose control is further underlined by the way that Eliza's rendition of 'Without You' is interrupted and abruptly terminated by Higgins as he proceeds to assert the first line of his song. The second number is potentially much more significant in its implications since, in a further, crucial reworking of the Pygmalion myth that is unique to Lerner and Loewe's musical adaptation of Shaw's play (the latter having ended sooner with Eliza bidding farewell to Higgins at his mother's house, telling him that he shall never see her again), Higgins is shown undergoing some form of emotional metamorphosis of his own as he sings 'I've Grown Accustomed To Her Face' during his walk back home. The extreme swings in tone that occur throughout this song (ranging from tender acknowledge-ments of how much Eliza has become part of his life to angry, vindictive speculations on the disastrousness to her of any marriage to Freddie (Jeremy Brett)) are crucial in conveying the emotional turbulence and struggle experienced by the male at this point as he alternatively confronts and resists his newly awakened feelings for Eliza.

But if this musical emphasis on the importance of the woman's voice – both to the expression of her own sense of selfhood and as a means of provoking change in the male – is indicative of certain progressive tendencies that link *My Fair Lady* to some of the musicals we will be look-ing at next, the manner in which the film then chooses to bring Eliza and Higgins back together again in the final scene raises questions about whether such positive developments can be sustained within the more 'realistic' spaces of the narrative world. The sequence in question occurs after Higgins is shown entering his house and follows on from a moment that further emphasises his sense of desolation at Eliza's departure. In what is perhaps the most poignant, convincing demonstration of Higgins' emotional change (containing, as it does, none of the more disturbing outbursts of aggression and misogyny that characterised his delivery of earlier songs), we are shown him trying to overcome his feelings of loss by playing a recording that he had made of Eliza's Cockney dialect during her first visit to his house. In a manner that seems markedly different from his earlier domination of Eliza through speech training, his reliance on this recorded version of her voice becomes, on this occasion, a manifestation of his emotional need and loss of control, the intentness with which he listens also conveying the impression of him listening to this pre-tutored, pre-manipulated version of her voice as if for the first time. It is at this point that Eliza returns unnoticed by him and, switching off the phonograph, says, in a reprisal of her former Cockney dialect: 'I washed my face and 'ands before I come, I did', while he, facing the camera and with his back to her, utters her name in surprise only to then recline back in his chair and, pushing his hat over his eyes in a snoozing pose, nonchalantly enquire: 'Where the devil are my slippers?'

Such a final exchange between the two main characters, endlessly debatable in terms of its implications, can be read at one extreme as a mark of the film's complex, mature handling of its subject matter or at the other as further proof of its ambivalence and confusion concerning Higgins and his treatment of Eliza. Avoiding the temptation to offer a more sentimental, cloying reunion of the couple, the film can be credited, to some extent, for the tentative, ironic manner in which it brings Eliza and Higgins together at the end, the effect of which is to leave open the question of their future viability as a romantic pair while also inviting speculation about the terms on which any such relationship would be founded. Yet there is something rather disquieting about the way that Eliza's words signal a retreat from her earlier display of vocal defiance as (eschewing Shaw's decision to end earlier with the female protagonist's declaration of independence) the film shows her announcing her return in a way that acknowledges her former class deference towards Higgins. Even more disconcerting, perhaps, is the way that Higgins in turn seeks to hide his pleasure at Eliza's return by using words that reinvoke his earlier authority over her, the implied instruction, inherent in his final line, for her to bring the slippers to him, also constituting a denial of his recently acknowledged feelings of admiration for the more defiant, independent Eliza. By granting us privileged access to Higgins' look of surprise on hearing her speak in person, the film seeks to convince us that his pleasure at her return is genuine but his ability to communicate such feelings directly to the female herself is something that his words and overall pose of indifference render uncertain.

The knowingness with which the two characters deliver their lines prevents us, of course, from reading their behaviour here as a simple, unquestioning return to their former roles. Indeed, this quality of self-consciousness can itself be regarded as a sign of Eliza's and Higgins' development by this stage in the narrative as they are shown signalling to each other an ironic awareness of the class and gender structures underpinning their earlier relationship and their sense of distance from their former roles. In Eliza's case, her response conveys a perhaps even deeper insight into Higgins' character as she seems to intuitively react to his unacknowledged feelings of loss and guilt by offering a verbal reassurance that this aspect of her identity has not altogether been destroyed. In Higgins' case, his final line is also open to an alternative reading for, in reinvoking the very words that triggered Eliza's rebellion on the night of the embassy ball (his enquiry about his slippers having prompted her on that occasion to throw them at him in anger), it could be construed not so much as an indication of his need to reassert his authority over her but as a teasing invitation for the more defiant Eliza to emerge.

The irony of such performances notwithstanding, though, the film ends by suggesting the characters' inability to come together and express their feelings for each other except through this re-enactment, however knowingly, of their former social roles. The qualified nature of the couple's reunion here can be highlighted by comparing *My Fair Lady*'s ending with the final section of *The Pirate*. Whereas that earlier film showed Serafin (Gene Kelly) and Manuela (Judy Garland) acting out their former roles (as Macoco the pirate and naïve female in love with this fantasy figure, respectively) in a way that seemed to serve mainly as a *prelude to* the more joyful abandonment of gender roles that takes place in the closing 'Be a Clown' number, *My Fair Lady* ends by leaving the characters frozen in this

ironic performance of their previous social roles. The static nature of Eliza and Higgins' poses, as they are shown framed in a stage-like tableaux, is particularly unpromising in this sense, raising questions as it does about their ability to move beyond this point. One could counter this by arguing that *The Pirate* is only able to achieve this more uninhibited release in the imaginary, illusion-filled world of entertainment and via the more anarchic mask of the clown. But the stasis characterising *My Fair Lady*'s ending also seems symptomatic of a more fundamental uncertainty on this film's part about how exactly the two main characters' relationship is to be construed. Whether one believes in these two characters' future as a romantic couple may also depend partly, of course, on whether one finds the pairing of Hepburn and Harrison sufficiently convincing in this regard.

So while *My Fair Lady* can be linked to the backstage musicals about the great female singer by virtue of its preoccupation with the unsettling impact of the woman's voice on the male protagonist, the equivocal nature of its ending tends to place certain limits on such a parallel. Whereas it toys with the possibility of the female bringing about some form of transformation in Higgins only to then qualify this by showing him hiding his newly awakened feelings for Eliza behind a pose of upper-class, male-chauvinist indifference, in these other films the destabilising effects of the great female singer on the male protagonist are generally the subject of much more sustained, extensive investigation, the tensions and anxieties generated by her voice seeming capable of provoking a much more extreme crisis in his identity. And if the concessions and compromises embodied in Eliza's final line of dialogue highlight some of the constraints placed on the woman's voice in *My Fair Lady* then this is doubly reinforced on a supra-filmic level. First, by the studio's decision not to cast Julie Andrews in the role that she herself had created on Broadway (thereby effacing this stronger female singing voice from the film altogether) and then by its strategy of dubbing (unbeknown to the actress herself)[2] Audrey Hepburn's voice with Marni Nixon's during the most musically demanding numbers in the film.

For those aware of this suppression of Hepburn's singing voice (and the availability of documentaries about the film's production history on DVD and elsewhere makes audience familiarity with this increasingly likely), the effect is particularly acute during the 'Rain in Spain', 'I Could Have Danced All Night' and 'Without You' numbers. In such cases, the utopianism of the songs is ironically undercut by our recognition that, at the very point where the female protagonist is supposed to discover her power of speech and self-expression, it is not, on a star level, the actual woman's voice that is allowed to be heard.[3] It is a scenario that links *My Fair Lady* to the next musical that we will be looking at, *Singin' in the Rain*, the plot of which is here uncannily enacted in actual production terms as Audrey Hepburn sings, unaware that her voice is to be dubbed by another woman.

Vocal theft and betrayal in Singin' in the Rain

Singin' in the Rain's witty account of the coming of sound era in Holly-wood acquires a particular relevance here due to its strategy of using the female voice – or, rather, two different kinds of female voice – to demon-strate both the difficulties and opportunities associated with the arrival of the talkies. In displaying this dual interest in the female voice, *Singin' in the Rain* therefore assumes a quite transitional place in this study. By centring its narrative on the raucous, uncouth speaking voice of the Jean Hagen character, Lina Lamont, on the one hand (a glamorous movie star of the silent era whose shrill, unsophisticated speaking voice now makes her a commercial liability to her studio), and the more talented singing voice of the Debbie Reynolds character, Kathy Selden, on the other (as the younger newcomer to the movies whose singing talent is deemed worthy of discovery), the film displays links both with *My Fair Lady* and with those backstage musicals about the great female singer that we will be consider-ing shortly.

In the first case, *Singin' in the Rain* clearly shares *My Fair Lady*'s con-cern with the disruptive potential of the lower-class female's speaking voice, the dissonant qualities of which again provide the motivation for various strategies of suppression and control. However in *Singin' in the Rain* this preoccupation is not tempered by any equivalent recognition of the cultural and musical value of such a voice nor by any sensitive aware-ness of the gender issues arising from its suppression. The film's own endorsement of the need to silence Lina's voice is made clear during the scene when, following a disastrous preview screening of her first talking picture with her co-star, Don Lockwood (Gene Kelly), the idea is hatched of turning that film ('The Duelling Cavalier') into a musical (later retitled as 'The Dancing Cavalier'). In showing how the europhia felt by Don, Kathy and Cosmo (Donald O'Connor) at this apparent solution – expressed through the trio's joyful performance of the song and dance number, 'Good Morning' – swiftly turns to disappointment as they realise the even greater unsuitability of Lina's voice for such an undertaking, the film presents this female's dissonant voice as a threat not just to her studio's first venture into talking pictures but to the birth of the movie musical itself.

And whereas *My Fair Lady* displays considerable sensitivity in high-lighting the sense of cultural displacement and alienation experienced by

Eliza following her transformation by Higgins, *Singin' in the Rain*'s decision to keep Lina in the dark about the studio's dubbing of Kathy's voice onto hers during Lina's musical and dialogue sections in 'The Dancing Cavalier' instead results in a narrative strategy of exclusion that seems designed to reinforce the Jean Hagen character's overall positioning as butt of the film's humour. Lina's recurring, indignant line of questioning – 'What do they/you think I am? Dumb or something?' – is the most obvious example of how the humour often works at her expense, the point of the joke being that in trying to convince them of her intelligence she only manages to demonstrate her lack of insight into her intellectual shortcomings. But the film's strategy of withholding other more crucial narrative information from her allows it to carry out a much more sustained chastisement of her character.

This conspiracy of exclusion begins with the sequence showing the first dubbing of Kathy's voice onto Lina's during the creation of the musical number 'Would You?' In a trio of shots held together by dissolves, the film presents first Kathy singing into the microphone, then Lina mangling the next section of the same song and, finally, Lina acting out her part in the final filmed version of the number, all the while oblivious to the fact that it is Kathy's voice that has replaced hers on the soundtrack. As a concise account of the mechanisms by which cinema can itself conspire in creating an illusion of ideal unity between female voice and image the sequence works quite effectively, with the final shot even managing to provide an implied response to an observation made earlier by one of the studio's employees: 'Lina, you're a beautiful woman. Audiences think you've got a voice to match.' However, any potential the film has for combining its amusing musical satire on the coming of sound with a more thoughtful examination of the status of the woman's voice in cinema is severely undermined by its portrayal of the Jean Hagen character both here and elsewhere. Treated as a comic grotesque figure, her voice (with its petulant, strident tones and frequent propensity for indulging in embarrassing verbal gaffes) is made to seem so out of tune (literally) with the film's musical project and pleasures as to discourage us from questioning the studio's decision to silence her.

And when she finally does discover that she is not going to be either singing or speaking for herself in the film and that Kathy is to receive full screen credit for her vocal role, her reaction of attempting to blackmail the studio head R.F. (Millard Mitchell) into agreeing to use the younger woman's voice in an uncredited capacity on this and future pictures only serves to vindicate the studio's attempts to withhold the dubbing from her. Her response is presented as so egotistical (deriving, as it does, from a deluded belief in the greatness of her own media-constructed star image) and so lacking in any sense of sisterhood as to negate or preclude any more positive potential inherent in this scenario where the woman (in a display of business acumen that counters her 'dumb blonde' image) stands up to the male-dominated structure of the studio and demands her right to speak. In showing Lina to be so ruthlessly willing to exploit Kathy's singing voice for the benefit of her own singing career, the film in turn manages to deflect attention and blame away from the studio and its readiness to manipulate both women's voices in order to ensure the financial success of their movie.

Lina's willingness to commit treachery against her vocal stand-in also provides the film with the necessary narrative justification it needs for her comic humiliation at the end. This occurs after the successful premiere of 'The Dancing Cavalier' when, having insisted on going out on stage to speak in person to her fans only to be then pressurised by the audience into singing live, Lina is exposed as a fraud by Cosmo, Don and R.F. Reassuring her that Kathy will again act as her voice by standing behind the curtain and singing for her while she (Lina) mimes the words, this trio of male characters then proceed (in another conspiracy against the Jean Hagen character) to lift the curtain mid-way through the number, thereby revealing the true source of the voice to a surprised movie audience whose ensuing roars of laughter drive Lina (permanently) and Kathy (temporarily) from the stage.

If the film's need to publicly humiliate Lina on stage in this way casts a shadow over the ending of this otherwise most high-spirited of Hollywood musicals, then it is also indicative, within the context of the present discussion, of *Singin' in the Rain*'s only limited allegiance to the backstage musicals about the great female singer. Although the discovery of the female's singing voice tends to rest in both cases on some chance occurrence or opportunity, in the case of *Singin' in the Rain* it is something that is only achievable through this invalidation of another's woman's voice. That Kathy's singing talents can only be recognised at the expense of this chastisement of the Jean Hagen character (a process that Michael Rogin sees as the product of 'the shift from ethnic to domestic conflict during and after the war' when, as he puts it, 'older career women like Lina Lamont were the scapegoats' (1996: 208)) is also a mark of the overall conservativeness of the film's utopian vision in gender terms. Its inability (unlike *My Fair Lady*) to contemplate the notion of the independent female with any degree of seriousness results in this scenario where, acting in collusion with the male characters, it finally allows Lina to speak for herself only so as to bring about her downfall.

Even if one accepts that this comic chastisement of Lina Lamont is justified by the film's wish to grant Kathy *her* independence from Lina's performing identity, its commitment to liberating the younger female singer from such ties is further compromised by the male characters' manipulation of her voice, as well, throughout the duration of this number. Like Lina, Kathy performs on stage unaware of her role in this male conspiracy, the similarity in the two female characters' position here being indicative of what Rogin regards as the film's unconscious doubling of these two women (ibid.). The gender structures and alignments at work during this

number are clearly highlighted by one particular shot taken from the theatre wings during Kathy's live dubbing of Lina's singing on stage. As Michel Chion observes, the significance of this shot lies in the way that it 'reveals the two women, one behind the other, with the two microphones lined up, both singing with this single voice that wanders between them looking for its source' while the three male characters, watching from the side of the stage, 'play at being the masters of the voice' (1999: 133).

This controlling male presence is also evident in the film's final sequence when, after Kathy has rushed off the stage in a state of distress, it is Don's voice that becomes the active, shaping force capable of bringing about both the recognition of her singing talent and the romantic reconciliation of the couple. Having called out to the audience to stop Kathy from running away, explaining that it was her voice that they heard in 'The Dancing Cavalier' and that she is 'the real star', Kelly's character thus proceeds to guide her back to the stage by singing a reprisal of the romantic number 'You Are My Lucky Star'. Having previously indicated, through the humiliation and expulsion of Lina Lamont, the chaos and self-destruction that ensues if the shrill-sounding woman is allowed to speak for herself, the film therefore concludes by only allowing even the more talented female singer to be recognised and validated through the medium of a controlling male voice.

One could argue, of course, that the figure of the guiding male who helps to bring the talented female newcomer to the audience's attention is a feature that the film shares with those backstage musicals about the great female singer. However, *Singin' in the Rain*'s allegiance to such films is limited both by the fairly passive nature of Kathy's role here (as she quickly complies by singing to Don the words of the song that he initiated) and by the uncomplicated wholesomeness of Debbie Reynolds' own singing voice. Lacking the greater strength and complex tonality associated with the singing voices of stars like Judy Garland, Doris Day and Barbra Streisand, it tends to reinforce, rather than resist, the conventionality of the female role allotted to Reynolds' character here. That Reynolds' voice was itself dubbed, both here and during the sequences where her character is supposed to be dubbing for Lina in 'The Dancing Cavalier',[4] ironically reinforces this sense of her voice being more susceptible to containment and control.

By way of demonstrating this point further, it is instructive to compare *Singin' in the Rain*'s ending with its counterpart in *Easter Parade* (Charles Walters, 1948). In that film the reconciliation of the couple at the end is brought about by a reversal (rather than an implied reassertion) of traditional gender roles as Hannah (Judy Garland) sings the film's title number to Don (Fred Astaire), having already appropriated the male convention (previously enacted in more typical form by Don at the beginning of the film) of sending flowers, together with an Easter hat and rabbit, to her lover. In providing such a noticeable contrast with *Singin' in the Rain*'s closing sequence, *Easter Parade*'s ending highlights how the presence of a stronger, more charismatic female singer may significantly disturb the gender power structures so characteristically inherent in the musical couple's romantic and professional relationship. In this particular instance, the privileging of Garland's voice in the final number even manages to overcome Astaire's more habitual mastery of the female through dance by the end of his films. Her active role as singer in turn facilitates a series of more detailed role reversals during the couple's impromptu dance in the male protagonist's apartment, with Garland even taking Astaire on her knee at one point while he responds throughout, as Babington and Evans observe in their close reading of the film, with a sense of 'embarrassment mixed with delight' as *he* 'is turned into the object of desire' (1985: 39).

Reconsidering the Pygmalion/Galatea and Svengali/Trilby narratives
in the light of the musical's fascination with the great female singer

Although we have identified certain distinctions between those musicals that deal with the female speaking voice and those centred on the great female singer, this is not to suggest that the latter group of films is somehow unproblematically free from the sort of pressures to contain and control the woman's voice that are to be found at work in *My Fair Lady* and *Singin' in the Rain*. Indeed, what *My Fair Lady* manages to highlight, through its adaptation of Shaw's play, is the extent to which the Pygmalion myth (so obviously at work in the kind of Ziegfeld tradition of musical spectacle that was parodied in *Funny Girl* and in the kind of Busby Berkeley style of production number that Fischer analyses) may also extend in the Hollywood musical to a concern on the part of the male mentor figure with the manipulation of the female voice. But whereas in *My Fair Lady* Eliza's speaking voice can only be properly celebrated once its more unruly, intrinsic qualities have been purged and her expression rechannelled through a more dominant upper-class, male discourse, in the musicals about the great female singer, the narratives are predicated, by contrast, on an intense, unwavering conviction in the uniqueness of the female singer's voice. Already fully-fledged at the point of discovery and never really in dispute or in need of improvement, this more talented voice is capable of commanding the instant respect and admiration of even the most demanding of male protagonists.

The Svengali/Trilby story (which, as noted earlier, provides a further important cultural backdrop to *My Fair Lady*) also constitutes another important literary influence on the Hollywood musical and one whose relevance to the films about the great female singer would seem particularly worthy of consideration given its central concern with the male protagonist's control of a woman's *singing* voice. The extent to which

Trilby's singing voice is both fashioned by and dependent on Svengali is demonstrated quite vividly in the 1931 film version of the novel during the sequence where the male protagonist's control over her begins to break down. In the final scene of this film (directed by Archie Mayo and retitled *Svengali*) we are shown how, as Svengali (John Barrymore) falls ill and begins to lose his hypnotic powers of concentration (as he stands conducting his wife's performance from his usual position as conductor in the orchestra pit), Trilby's singing begins to falter and deteriorate before then stopping altogether as she (Marian Marsh) clutches her throat in surprise, the potential freedom that his death offers her being swiftly thwarted by his final request for her to follow him.

Yet whereas Trilby's voice has to be more or less completely refashioned by Svengali in order for her to become a successful concert singer, in the musicals about the great female singer, the woman's voice tends to be much more resistant to male control. According to Edward Turk Baron, Jeanette MacDonald offers one particularly notable instance of where the trained soprano is able to use her voice to exert a significant power and authority in film. While noting how her voice tended to be more tightly regulated and contained within the 'exceedingly male-dominated, logocentric world' of the romantic comedies she made with Maurice Chevalier (1994: 105), he argues that it was given much freer rein in the musicals she made with Nelson Eddy. In such cases, 'the unleashing of MacDonald's soprano and its coupling with Eddy's baritone work to deflate phallic authority and to impose a decidedly feminine imprint on their films' (ibid.). For Baron, this 'deployment of a cinematically powerful voice' (1994: 104) (with all the excess and intensity of feeling that it is able to convey) provides the key to understanding MacDonald's ability to generate extremely diverse visceral responses in the American public. Summarising the historical reception of her films with Eddy, he points out how these at first provoked 'an initial period of mass adulation' before then becoming 'subject to virtually unparalleled extremes of parody and disparagement' (1994: 103). Using MacDonald as his case study, Baron argues that 'the capacity of sopranos to provoke intense pleasure and displeasure' (1994: 111) – particularly in the *male* movie-going public – can be explained in psychoanalytic terms.

On the one hand, he maintains, the soprano's voice is able to reinvoke the pleasures of infantile union with the mother; its feminine, lyrical qualities capable of recalling, on this reading, the foetus' first auditory experience of the mother's voice while in the womb together with other soothing instances of the maternal voice (such as the lullaby) during infancy. At the same time, he argues, the soprano's voice also has the capacity to reawaken repressed fears and anxieties arising from the male child's separation from the mother, the high-pitched nature of such singing in this sense recalling 'the strident infantile scream (signifying lack and helplessness)' (1994: 113) that is emitted by him at the moment of birth. Developing this line of thought further, Baron argues that if 'the intensity of sound MacDonald produces (especially at climaxes) and the progressive heightening of her vocal range throughout the 1930s (resulting in relative obfuscation of words to the advantage of musical line) reactivate the hallucinatory pleasures of acoustic omnipotence associated with prelinguistic, infantile narcissism', then, 'For moviegoers otherwise disposed, these same factors generate anxiety and embarrassment. At issue in both dispositions', Baron suggests, 'is the moviegoer's willingness to accept or to disavow the maternal voice as the agency of acoustic authority' (1994: 112). Whether one accepts the psychoanalytic basis of Baron's explanations is, of course, a matter for debate but, in focusing on the cinematic power of the female singing voice, his article provides a provocative attempt to think through an area of the musical that has been unjustly ignored. Indeed, for Baron, the critical neglect of MacDonald's films is itself indicative of this need to repress and disavow both the potency of the female voice and the male's dependency on it for his own sense of subjectivity.

Where the analysis offered here departs most crucially of all from Baron's is in its conviction that it is the great female singer of American popular song rather than the more classically-trained soprano who tends, overall, to be invested with the most sustained and complex subversive charge in the Hollywood musical. The individual, one-off nature of this kind of voice is reinforced by its equation with a form of music that itself carries powerful associations of freedom, self-expression and spontaneity (for a discussion of the musical's tendency to privilege popular song over classical music, see Feuer 1993: 49–65). Hence, while there are several other cycles of musical films (from the 1930s, 1940s and 1950s especially) whose narratives deal with the figure of the gifted female soprano (often starring the likes of Grace Moore, Kathryn Grayson and, of course, Jeanette MacDonald and usually focusing on a triangular relationship involving the female singer, a young man who was an earlier boyfriend/supporter of hers and an older male impresario figure who is more influential and can help her career), it is one particularly enduring group of backstage musicals dealing with the great female singer of American popular song that this study is most concerned with. So while Jeanette MacDonald's performance in *San Francisco* (W. S. Van Dyke, 1936) forms a significant part of the discussion, much of the analysis centres on how her voice achieves its greatest impact at that moment when she applies her operatic voice to a full-throttle rendition of the film's popular title song, the effect of which completely outstrips anything that the male protagonist had managed to achieve when showing her how to sing the same song earlier at his club.

Given the stronger power of the great female singer's voice it is perhaps not surprising, then, that where the Svengali influence manifests itself most clearly in these films is in their depiction of the male protagonist as a quite troubled, angst-ridden character for whom the desire to control the woman's singing appears both symptomatic of some previously existing insecurity on his part and a source of immense pressure and strain. Indeed, just as John Barrymore's Svengali is shown becoming increasingly ill the greater the control he exerts over Trilby (to the point where his desire for mastery actually kills him) then so in these musicals does the male mentor figure often display some analogous physical sign of his insecurity. And if Svengali at times displays an ironic awareness of the futility of his control ('Ah, you are beautiful, my manufactured love. But it is only Svengali talking to himself again' he observes wryly on witnessing Trilby declare her fake love for him while under the influence of hypnosis), in a film like *A Star is Born* (George Cukor, 1954) the male protagonist becomes endowed with an even more tragic insight into the destructiveness of the influence he exerts over his singing protégée.

The complexity of these films thus seems to lie precisely in their ability to rework the Pygmalion and Svengali stories in ways that take into account the more uncontainable force of the great female singer's voice, the influence of which has a tendency to spill out beyond the parameters of the numbers themselves and into the narrative world as a whole. This complexity is also reflected in the generic hybridity of these films, most of which tend to combine the more liberating, utopian potential of the musical form with such darker generic elements as the biopic, gangster and even disaster movie format. As we shall see, this hybrid quality is crucial to the expression of the films' gender concerns, with the tensions between the various generic elements being symptomatic of the conflicts and disturbances arising from the presence within these narrative worlds of a more potent vocal force. Indeed, if the presence of a strong, charismatic female singing voice in a musical like *Easter Parade* manages to produce a quite pleasurable destabilisation of gender structures, in those generically hybrid musicals dealing with the female singer's involvement with a non-singing or non-dancing male, the resulting imbalance in their relationship often tends to provoke a more traumatic set of gender-related tensions and anxieties.

San Francisco

San Francisco is an instructive case in point as this is a film which combines the backstage musical with the disaster movie in its depiction of the fraught relationship between a young aspiring opera singer, Mary Blake (Jeanette MacDonald), and the owner of a nightclub, Blackie Norton (Clark Gable), in the months leading up to the famous real-life earthquake of 1906. In that film, the power of the female singing voice is demonstrated most vividly during the scene where Mary tries to help Blackie (from whom she is at this point estranged but still in love with) by representing his Paradise Club at a talent competition at the annual Chicken's Ball. Although by now a successful opera singer, having left Blackie and her job as a singer in his club for the second time, Mary offers to sing on behalf of his establishment here on discovering, just moments before, that her fiancé Jack Burley (Jack Holt), a member of the San Francisco aristocracy and political as well as romantic rival to Blackie, has had her former lover's club raided on a gambling charge and all of his performers (due to appear at the ball) thrown into jail.

But Mary's ability to win the contest single-handedly with a rousing rendition of the film's title number proves too much of a threat to Blackie's male ego and pride. Arriving at the ball just in time to hear her announced as the winner, he walks on stage and, refusing her offer to represent his club, throws the trophy and prize money onto the floor. Highly self-destructive in professional terms, his response seems to be motivated not just by feelings of romantic rejection and political rancour but also by a need to refuse the very different conditions by which their relationship is now being defined. For while Mary still sings here out of a sense of indebtedness to Blackie for giving her a start to her career (a sense of obligation that had earlier enabled him to keep her at his club despite her receiving a second offer to sing at the Tivoli Opera), now she does so as an independent, successful performer in her own right and, even more crucially, in a way that this time threatens to make *him* beholden to *her*. And whereas Mary's first rendition of the 'San Francisco' number had earlier provided Blackie with an opportunity to exert his authority over her during her first rehearsal at his club ('Put something into it! Heat it up! That's what it's about – San Francisco!' he told her then), on this occasion her delivery of the song takes place without his knowledge (Gable's character having left the club moments before) and is performed with a versatility that now allows her to give equal weight to both the popular and operatic sides of her singing identity. In combining these two styles of singing within one performance, MacDonald's character is able to achieve a fluid, flexible style of vocal expression that contrasts quite markedly with Blackie's intransigent display of male pride later on and in a way that also constitutes an emphatic rejection of Burley's earlier, equally uncompromising order for her not to perform.

Blackie's inability to cope with this stronger, more independent assertion of the female singer's voice had also manifested itself earlier on in the film when, stung by her first departure from his club, he arrived at the Tivoli Opera intent on halting her debut performance. On that occasion his resentment was temporarily quelled on hearing her sing at the packed opera house, his absorption in her performance causing him to forget his original motive for being there and even prompting him to knock out the bailiff as this official tries to serve the prohibition order that he (Blackie) had instigated. That Blackie's reform is only temporary is made clear in the very next scene in Mary's dressing room when his agreement to marry her is shown to be conditional on her giving up her independent career at the opera and returning to sing at his club. The key difference between these two scenes, however, is that whereas on that occasion Blackie had sought to stop her from singing *anywhere else* but at the Paradise Club, now he is shown refusing to allow her to sing *for* his club. It is a shift in his position that reflects the much greater threat that her singing now poses to his sense of male authority and control. And unlike what happened during the earlier scene at the opera, Blackie's resentment of Mary's growing autonomy as a performer goes unchecked by the positive transformative impact of her singing, his inability to intervene and silence her voice now arising from his *absence* throughout her performance of the 'San Francisco' number rather than from any more voluntary acquiescence to its charms. Given Blackie's growing inability to cope with the independent strength and status of the female singer's voice it is interesting to bear in mind that, according to Baron, 'Clark Gable, MGM's quintessential man's man, initially balked at co-starring with MacDonald in *San Francisco* ... on the grounds that "all he would have to do was stand there while Jeanette sang, not *his* idea of a good picture"' (1994: 113).

The fact that the earthquake follows on immediately after this incident at the Chicken Ball (the first tremors occur just as Mary begins to leave the building) endows *San Francisco*'s key disaster event with a more subversive meaning than that encouraged by the film's explicit moral agenda. The latter, voiced most notably by the priest Father Tim Mullin (Spencer Tracy) and by Maisie Burley (Jessie Ralph), the mother of Mary's fiancé, encourages us to read the earthquake as an Old Testament-style punishment of the city for its decline into sin and corruption. But the precise timing of this seismic disaster enables us to construe it rather differently as a metaphorical dramatisation of the power of this female singer's voice to destabilise the masculine structures of control implicit in her relationship with Blackie and (to a lesser extent) Burley. In a manner that both anticipates and invites comparison with the impact of the earthquake on the evening's proceedings, the Jeanette MacDonald character succeeds in 'bringing the house down' and in a way that is capable of provoking considerable emotional turbulence in the male protagonist himself. In generic terms, therefore, one could argue that the gender tensions and pressures generated by the female singer's voice during this key musical moment are displaced onto and in turn resolved through the disaster movie plot, with the eruption of the earthquake at first providing a further but indirect outlet for such concerns before then (in provoking Blackie's search for Mary) facilitating a reconciliation of the couple.

Having initially served as a metaphorical expression of the disruptive power of the female singing voice, then, the earthquake ultimately acts as a means by which the film is able to defuse its more threatening aspects. For as the city lies in a state of devastation in the final scene, it is the regenerative, healing capacity of MacDonald's singing (what Baron would presumably refer to as the nurturingly maternal rather than castrating or trauma-inducing potential of the soprano voice) that now becomes most prominent. In keeping with the film's somewhat repressive need to purge San Francisco of its moral impurities (a process that requires the city that is described in the prologue as 'sensuous, vulgar and magnificent' to be replaced with one that is 'industrious, mature, respectable'), MacDonald's hymn-singing (so different in tone and content from her earlier celebration of San Francisco) is what helps bring about some form of religious conversion in the self-confessed atheist Blackie who, moved to tears by this spectacle of her singing among the ruins, is shown kneeling down and giving thanks to God.

In broader terms, too, her hymn-singing is now construed quite patriotically as a force capable of inspiring the people of the city to *overcome* the devastating effects of the earthquake, a meaning that is reinforced by the film's closing dissolve from a shot showing the old San Francisco in ruins to one depicting the new, rebuilt version of the city. Yet while MacDonald's singing is enlisted in the service of this more conservative ideological project, the film still manages to end with a remarkably intense demonstration of the female singer's enduring vocal strength. Indeed, in celebrating her ability to survive and even prosper in a situation of such extreme adversity, *San Francisco*'s ending provides one of the most striking and unashamedly sentimental illustrations of the Hollywood musical's belief in the resilience of the female singer. It is this quality of vocal resilience which is the force capable of inspiring a profound sense of renewal not just in the city but within the male protagonist himself.

Having established the importance of the female singer's voice – both as a way of articulating complex matters of gender identity and as a force capable of destabilising some of the traditional power structures and assumptions underpinning her relationship with a controlling male figure – we will now explore how these tendencies are developed much more fully in a trio of musicals about the 'great female singer', the complexity of which derives precisely from their readiness to confront this question of what happens when the woman sings.

Love Me or Leave Me

Love Me or Leave Me (Charles Vidor, 1955) is the first of three films we will be looking at that seek to explore in much more extreme, harrowing form, the problems and traumas experienced by the female singer as she strives for success within the often far from glamorous world of the backstage musical. In this case, the film's uncompromising perspective on its subject matter is heightened by the way that it combines this darker 'backstage' element with both the biopic genre (the film is based on the life of Ruth Etting, a real-life torch singer who rose to fame during the 1920s in America) and the gangster movie. The latter connection is evoked by the film's location of its narrative world in Chicago during the 1920s and, more importantly, by the casting of former gangster star James Cagney in the role of Marty Snyder, a ruthless laundry racketeer who becomes Etting's domineering manager and husband. The darker edge arising from Cagney's presence in the film is made clear during his very first appearance, the expressionist-style shot showing his silhouette looming up on the wall as his character enters the nightclub where Etting works serving to herald the introduction of a more volatile, menacing figure into the world of the backstage musical. Although Cagney made films in a number of different genres, including the musical, it is his image as a tough-talking but charismatic hoodlum figure whose fighting approach is inextricably bound up with his working-class identity that *Love Me or Leave Me* trades on most. The fact that Cagney's persona of working-class toughness often extended to his characters' treatment of women (a point demonstrated most famously by that moment in *The Public Enemy* (William Wellman, 1931) where Cagney pushes a grapefruit into Mae Clarke's face) is something that the film both draws upon and seeks to challenge through its depiction of Snyder's relationship with Etting.

The casting of Doris Day in the role of Ruth Etting provides a crucial counterpoint to Cagney's performance in this respect. By foregrounding her character's stubborn resistance to Snyder's attempts to manipulate her, the film makes use of an aspect of her star persona that was arguably far more complex than the stereotyped images of her as 'Constant Virgin' or 'Girl Next Door' (for feminist reappraisals of Doris Day's star image, see Clarke *et al.* 1980 and 1981). It is an aspect of Day's star persona that the film makes a point of stressing during her first appearance in the same opening scene at the 'ten cents a dance' nightclub. On that occasion she was shown resisting a male customer's attempts to grope her during a dance and then angrily protesting on being fired by her boss. Such defiance is what ironically brings her to the attention of Snyder who uses his contacts to get her a job as a dancer at another nightclub.

The chief irony played on by the film, though, is that while Etting regards her singing talent as a means of escaping her sexual exploitation as a dancer, she ultimately ends up becoming subject to another form of prostitution in her relationship with the Cagney character. The film unsentimentally presents Etting herself as implicated to some extent in these structures of exploitation and uses the character of Johnny Alderman (Cameron Mitchell), her musical arranger and alternative love interest, to suggest how she is blinding herself to the implications of using Snyder to advance her career until it is too late to free herself from his control. (That Alderman himself is not altogether beyond reproach is made clear by the parallels invited between him and Snyder, both of whose offers of help are sexually motivated.) And when she finally does give in to Snyder's sexual claims on her by agreeing to marry him (the key scene here being the one where Snyder, outraged at his eviction from Ziegfeld's theatre on the grounds of bad behaviour, first threatens to pull her out of the show and then, tormenting her with reminders of what he has done for her, forces himself on her), the film makes plain her sense of having prostituted herself: 'You don't have to sell me. I'm sold' she tells Snyder following the disclosure of their marriage.

This stark acknowledgement of the sexual economics underpinning her relationship to Snyder even extends to the musical numbers themselves. It finds most explicit expression in the song 'Ten Cents a Dance', the first full-length number that Etting is shown performing after her marriage to Snyder and following her withdrawal from the Ziegfeld show. Positioned at such a point in the narrative and with its clear allusions to her earlier job as a nightclub dancer (ten cents was the fee that the male customers paid to dance with her), this number highlights the extent to which Etting sees herself as still trapped within the same crude forms of sexual exploitation that she found so oppressive at the start of her career.

But while Etting's marriage to Snyder is accompanied by a loss of self-will on her part as she is shown becoming apathetic about her career as he continues to dictate her every professional move, the film insists on the importance of the act of singing in enabling her to retain a sense of selfhood during even the most extreme moments of personal despair. Thus, if the song 'Ten Cents a Dance' musically reinforces, on one level, her resigned sense of having sold herself to Snyder, this is complicated and challenged by the active, intense nature of Doris Day's performance during this number. The impassioned style of the singer's vocal delivery and the strong, confident posture she adopts throughout (as she stands, hands on hips, her feet pointed assertively outwards) combine to convey a much more defiant stance of resistance on her character's part.

Similarly, during her first reunion with Johnny in Hollywood, her delivery of the song 'I'll Never Stop Loving You' during a private rehearsal in one of the recording studios offers her a momentary respite from her otherwise defeatist state of mind, her display of indifference to Johnny's choice of song giving way to a performance of great intensity and commitment and one that prompts the arranger to remark afterwards: 'Yes, you still care about it.' The recording studio therefore becomes an important performing space wherein Ruth is able to rediscover her sense of autonomy from Snyder. And while this process of recovery takes place in the presence of another, albeit more benign male mentor figure, the camera's strategy of isolating Day in the frame at certain points during her singing suggests, together with the sense of self-absorption conveyed by her delivery of this  particular song, that there is an aspect of her character's being to which such moments give expression that even he cannot influence or access.

As Etting recovers her sense of self-worth then so, conversely (and in a manner that anticipates the two films that we will be looking at next), do Snyder's insecurities begin to surface as his control over her becomes weakened by her increasing success and autonomy as a performer. This process is registered in spatial terms by Snyder's increasing exclusion from the performing arenas of first the New Amsterdam theatre on Broadway and then the sound recording stage in Hollywood. Snyder's response, in the first instance, is to force his way backstage during Etting's opening night performance. However, while, like his male counterpart in *San Francisco*, Snyder attempts to regain control over the female singer by intruding into a sphere of entertainment much grander than what he is used to (the equivalent in Blackie's case being the scene where he visits the Tivoli Opera intent on halting Mary's debut performance), in Snyder's case his behaviour is much more fraught with insecurity about his own status (in both class and gender terms) and much more emotionally damaging in its implications for the female herself.

Snyder's insecurities are heightened during the later sections of the film as he is forced to confront (in ways that effectively pick up where *San Francisco*, at the point of the earthquake, left off) the extent to which his identity has become defined in relation to the female singer. This process is triggered, appropriately, by Ruth's striking vocal intervention during the scene where Snyder is shown giving an account of his initial meeting with the head of the studio that Ruth is contracted to for her first picture. Having excluded Ruth from that meeting (an absence that he had earlier explained to Hunter (Richard Gaines) in the following terms: 'Mrs Snyder just sings. I'm the one that does the talking.') he then boasts to her about how he handled the studio head. On this occasion, his macho posturing proves too much for Ruth who, relinquishing her more usual stance of silent resignation, interrogates him in a manner that leaves him visibly shaken:

Marty:	I really let him have it, didn't I Barney? That's the only way with those phonies. You've gotta let them know who you are.
Ruth:	Who are you, Marty?
Marty:	[After a pause] What do you mean?
Ruth:	What have you accomplished? Can you produce a picture? Have you done one successful thing on your own? Just who do you think you are?

For those familiar with accounts of Doris Day's own troubled personal life, such moments arguably take on an added biographical charge due to the similarities that have sometimes been drawn between Etting's relationship to Snyder and Day's marriage (in 1951) to her manager Marty Melcher (who also coincidentally shared the same first name as Cagney's character). Commenting on this in his biography of Doris Day, Eric Braun observes that: 'Cagney also saw the parallel between the relationship of Ruth Etting and Martin Snyder and Doris Day and Marty Melcher:

he thought that both [men] lived vicariously through their wives' lives' (2004: 143–4).

Although Cagney's character tries, for his part, to recover his poise by reasserting his claim (also made by Higgins in *My Fair Lady* along with a host of other Pygmalion/Svengali-style male figures in the Hollywood musical) that he 'made' her what she is: 'Whoever I am kiddo, I'm what makes you tick and don't you ever forget that', her words find independent reinforcement elsewhere from his loyal sidekick Georgie (Harry Bellaver). While attempting to placate Snyder, this character only serves to make the implications of her speech even more explicit:

> Listen, Marty. I figure I get what she means. Back in Chicago, you were a big man, see. But since then, the people we do business with, your name don't mean nothing. After all, it ain't like it's up anywhere: 'Marty Snyder Presents'. Sure, you're married to her. But for all they know, you could be a guy that's hanging onto a good thing – a meal ticket. Do you follow what I mean, Marty?

Snyder's response of punching Georgie consequently appears as an attempt to reassert a male ego now seriously undermined by these two moments, both of which, in reversing his own assumption about Ruth's indebtedness to him, force him to confront a perception of himself that he had not previously countenanced. It is a realisation that seems to awaken in him a deep-seated insecurity about his male identity. Such insecurity was alluded to right from the outset, in fact, in the form of Snyder's insistent limp, a physical impairment that (earning him the title of 'the Gimp') even precedes his involvement with Ruth. But if his efforts to take control of her career at the beginning of the film and make her a success can in one sense be read as an attempt to compensate for some previously existing male anxieties on his part, her success only ends up fuelling such insecurities even further by threatening to subsume his identity into hers. Snyder's response is to attempt to assert an independent identity of his own through the purchase and renovation of a nightclub which he then names (after his initials) 'The MS Club'. This use of the club to bolster his threatened sense of identity even extends to his design of the decor which excessively bears his initials everywhere (at one point he is shown giving instructions for the crockery to have the letters 'MS' printed on them).

This use of the club to shore up his insecure masculinity is itself threatened, though, by Snyder's discovery that Ruth is romantically involved with her musical arranger. The state of confusion that this throws Snyder into is suggested by the self-destructive, contradictory way in which he responds. Not only is he shown smashing a whole stack of wine glasses in his club at one point, but he also threatens to pull Ruth out of the picture she is working on with Johnny and make her sing at his place. While Snyder clearly issues this threat in an attempt to recover his sense of control over her ('You're going to work here. You're going to open this joint. And there's going to be a sign: "Martin Snyder Presents Ruth Etting" – that way everybody'll know who's boss', he tells her), in countering his earlier wish of not allowing her to have anything to do with this new venture of his, his directive only further underlines his inability to assert his independence from her.

If Snyder's shooting of Alderman represents a last desperate attempt to reassert his masculinity then this action of his also involves an unleashing of Cagney's gangster persona in more extreme form. Yet while this demonstration of a more ruthless, volatile side to Cagney's persona is used here to highlight the problematic nature of Snyder's masculinity (and in a way that poses some threat to the film's ability to resolve itself as a musical), in the subsequent scenes at the prison and nightclub, Cagney's gangster persona is employed in ways that, enabling the film to now move towards some form of narrative resolution, seem designed to shore up the male protagonist's embattled ego. This is particularly evident during the scene at the prison where the assertion of a more belligerent persona is part of the means by which the film allows Cagney's character to recover his male pride. Indeed, when Snyder tells Ruth (in an attempt to shrug off the indignities of his imprisonment) during her visit to him in jail: 'Tell him [Johnny] I like it. Makes me feel like I'm a kid again', it is almost as if, now located within a setting so redolent of his earlier movies, Cagney is proclaiming, with characteristic defiance, his pleasure at this rejuvenation of his more youthful, rebellious screen persona.

A further challenge to Snyder's identity comes, though, in the final scene when, on being released from jail on bail, he returns to his nightclub only to find that its survival (seriously jeopardised by his imprisonment and impending trial) has been ensured by Ruth's decision to perform there. The full significance of Ruth's gesture is worth dwelling on here. For while the flashing neon sign that greets the Cagney character on his arrival at the club – 'MARTIN SNYDER PRESENTS RUTH ETTING' – in one sense constitutes a fulfilment of his earlier threat to make her perform there and while Ruth's decision to sing is itself motivated by strong feelings of indebtedness towards him, by choosing to perform of her own accord she now takes (for the first time) active control over her voice and in a way that confirms without doubt *his* dependency on her. As in *San Francisco*, where the woman also chose, out of similar motives, to use her singing voice in an attempt to rescue another male whose club had fallen into a precarious situation, the female protagonist's gesture here provokes an outburst of resentment in the male himself as he is forced to confront the extent of his reliance on her (in this case, for the success of the very venture that was originally intended to prove his independence from her). On this occasion, though, the male's resentment is quelled not by the dramatic device of an earthquake but by the diplomatic words of agent Barney Loomis (Robert Keith) who deftly reconstrues the situation in ways that make Snyder's *acceptance*, rather than rejection, of the woman's offer of help a proof of his manhood:

> Now listen to me. This is not a handout. You did a lot for Ruth in the old days. She knows it and she's grateful and she's got a right to pay it back. And you've got to take it. You've got to be big enough to take it.

Boosted by the attention he receives from some inquisitive reporters (his witty repartee with them providing further opportunities for a display of Cagney's cocky, defiant persona) but then faltering at the doorway as he notices Ruth's singing, Snyder's resistance is gradually overcome when, having initially seated himself at the bar with his back to the stage in a posture that signals his unwillingness to acknowledge her presence, he looks first at his initials on one of the ashtrays and then around at his club. As if reassured by these signifiers of his status, he finally arrives at a more objective appreciation of Ruth's talents as a singer, complimenting her in a manner that, while still ultimately construed in ways that seem designed to shore up his own ego, no longer appears governed by the ulterior sexual motives that underpinned his earlier gestures of help. Turning around to face her as she performs, he says to Loomis with a noticeable degree of pride: 'You've got to give her credit. The girl can sing. About that, I never was wrong.'

The final shot showing Ruth performing the title number on stage captures both the tensions inherent in her relationship with Snyder at this point and the complexity of the gender identity issues at stake. In purely

visual terms, the camera's tracking back away from the stage to reveal a large version of Snyder's club insignia (a wreath bearing the initials 'M.S.') embroidered on one of the curtain drapes hanging above Ruth's head would seem to insist on Snyder's continuing oppressive influence over her, the weight of his persona appearing to bear down on her even at the very point where she seeks to absolve her debt to him. Yet in musical terms, it is the female's act of singing which is sustaining this bombastic display of Snyder's identity. Indeed, as the camera tracks back away from the stage, it is as if it responds to and is even buoyed up by the trajectory of the woman's voice as Day's singing expands effortlessly outwards into the auditorium. The fluid, mobile properties of the female singer's voice and the assured, relaxed nature of the delivery offer a striking aural counterpoint to the forced, overbearing masculinity inherent in the *mise-en-scène*, indicating an ability on the part of the character herself to break free from the confines of the male identity represented in such static, circumscribed terms, by the sign above her.

A Star is Born

George Cukor's *A Star is Born* (the second of three film versions of this story) is another musical that deals with the female singer's fraught, intense relationship with a male figure who (in this case in his role as an established movie actor) comes to exert a considerable influence over her as he helps to transform her career from singer in a band to successful star of musical pictures. This basic scenario is complicated considerably by *A Star is Born*'s preoccupation with both the regenerative and oppressive effects of the female singer's voice on the male as he first discovers and then becomes increasingly swamped by her singing talent. Indeed, if *Love*

Me or Leave Me went further than *San Francisco* in the latter respect by directly confronting the violent, destructive consequences arising from the male's resentment of the female singer's success (consequences that *San Francisco* could only deal with indirectly through the devastating device of the earthquake), then *A Star is Born* in turn goes much further than *Love Me or Leave Me* in its depiction of the crisis experienced by the male as he seeks to come to terms with his growing dependency on the woman for his own status and identity.

It is instructive in this respect to compare the scene in *A Star is Born* where the out-of-work Norman Maine (James Mason) goes to the races, having just been successfully treated for his alcoholism at a clinic, only to be then taunted by his former publicity manager Libby (Jack Carson) about his financial dependency on Esther (Judy Garland), with the one in *Love Me or Leave Me* where Georgie points out to Marty that people could be thinking that he (Marty) is using Ruth as 'a meal ticket'. Both scenes provide pivotal moments where the male is forced to confront an unflattering perception of his relationship to the female singer. But in Norman's case, the experience proves much more humiliating for although, like Snyder, he tries to recover his male pride by punching the person concerned, on this occasion it results in him being knocked to the floor in a very public setting and by a hostile figure who, unlike Georgie, has no desire to be considered his friend. And whereas the threat posed to Snyder's identity finds some compensation or relief in his use of the 'MS Club' to bolster his image and, in star terms, through the reassertion of Cagney's cocky, defiant gangster persona towards the end of the film, the equivalent incident in *A Star is Born* triggers Norman's relapse into alcoholism and his eventual suicide.

Norman's decline appears all the more sympathetic given the greater generosity and insight that he displays with regard to the female singer's talent than does his counterpart in *Love Me or Leave Me*. Whereas Marty's interest in Ruth's singing only arose after an initial spell of indifference and even then only in an attempt to solicit sexual favours from her, Norman's appreciation of Esther's singing is presented as much more sincere and immediately forthcoming. Indeed, unlike Marty – who can only arrive at a more objective, impartial acknowledgement of Ruth's talents right at the end of *Love Me or Leave Me* – Norman is able to acknowledge his regard for Esther's talent freely and openly from the outset. Having thanked her for her professional handling of his drunken intrusion on stage during her number at the Shrine auditorium (a display of indebtedness itself unthinkable in either Blackie's or Marty's case), Norman proceeds to extol Esther's talent even more profusely on hearing her sing 'The Man That Got Away' during the scene at the Downbeat Club. Having then offered to arrange a screen test for her during their conversation at her boarding house, he leaves her with the following words of encouragement: 'Whether you do it or not, don't ever forget how good you are. Hang onto that.' Although his attempt to back this up with the assertion – 'Because I'm right' – invites some comparison with Marty's corresponding claim at the end of *Love Me or Leave Me*: 'You've got to give her credit, the girl can sing. *About that, I never was wrong*', on this occasion the male's insistence on the correctness of his judgement appears genuinely motivated by a desire to convince the female singer of her talent rather than by a self-satisfied wish to bolster his own ego.

Norman's status as a highly complex, sympathetic male mentor figure also stems from the way that his appreciation of Esther's singing seems to bring about a much more sincere emotional commitment to this female than anything alluded to in his previous relationships with women, the superficiality of which was made clear during the scene where he visits the Coconut Grove in search of Esther. The ability of Esther's singing to provoke some form of important emotional reawakening in Norman is sug-gested quite literally during the scene where he is woken up, rejuvenated, from his drunken slumbers by the recollection of the song that she performed during their first encounter on stage at the Shrine auditorium. Such a metamorphosis in the male (hinted at right at the beginning of the sequence through the shot showing the actor's shirt lying discarded, chrysalis-like, on the floor) finds further expression during the scene at the boarding house. On that occasion, Norman's words of encouragement (having just heard her sing for a second time) are rounded off by a sequence that highlights the change that her singing has wrought on his way of seeing. Having just said goodnight to Esther who turns and begins to walk away, Norman suddenly calls out 'Hey!' before adding more softly, on seeing her turn around in surprise: 'I just want to take another look at you.'

Although displaying some signs of Norman's influence over Esther (note, for example, how he signals that he has finished looking at her by waving her away in a manner that prompts the singer to bow somewhat deferentially in response), this moment seems to be motivated much more importantly by a newfound recognition of the individuality of this particular female image, the full complexity and distinctiveness of which he thus seeks to capture and hold in his memory. Indeed, to read Norman's look here as simply a demonstration of the power of the male gaze would be to ignore the tenderness with which Mason both delivers his lines and looks at Garland's character at this point. That Norman should again call Esther back and reaffirm his wish to look at her once more just before going down to the beach to commit suicide near the end of the film is also significant for it makes clear how his entire relationship with her is framed by this much more mature, emotionally profound way of looking. These two rhyming moments invite striking contrast with the sequence where, as Esther emerges from the church fol-

lowing Norman's funeral, she is confronted by one of her female fans who, insisting that she 'give us just one look', pulls the veil away to reveal Garland's grief-stricken face. Although itself motivated by feelings of adoration, this act of tearing away the veil constitutes a valuation of Esther's star identity that carries no corresponding respect for the integrity of her inner self. The assertion of the right to look consequently results in this instance in a violation of the woman's image that (in a reversal of the more positive voice/image/identity dialectic discussed earlier with regard to Norman) provokes a traumatic scream of protest from Garland herself.

This respect for the integrity of Esther's image finds further expression in Norman's rejection of the studio's attempt (prior to her first audition) to create a more glamorous look for her and in his insistence on restoring her former appearance to her. On taking her back to his dressing room, he consequently sets about reversing the effects of her long session at the studio's make-up department. 'Now, take every bit of that junk off your face ... then put on your eyebrows and your lipstick the way you always

do and I'll do the rest...' he tells her before adding (in an attempt to allevi-ate her insecurity about her physical imperfections and having just covered her face in white make-up remover cream): 'Your face is just dandy.' In his dismissal of the studio's attempt to refashion Esther's image accord-ing to some male-constructed ideal of female beauty and in his concern with reasserting the woman's notion of how she should look, Norman acts here in a way that serves to place him in a much more oppositional position with regard to the Pygmalion myth. Although still acting very much in the tradition of the

guiding male mentor figure whose influence proves crucial in transform-ing the female singer's career, he does so in a manner that now seems much more committed to the idea of allowing the woman's own identity to emerge. His understanding of the importance of Esther's singing to the expression of her selfhood is encapsulated in the advice he gives her, just before she goes for her audition: 'Look, forget the camera. It's the Downbeat Club at 3 o'clock in the morning and you're singing for yourself and the boys in the band. *Mainly for yourself, the way I heard you.*'

It is this respect for the woman's autonomy of self that also makes him, unlike the other male figures we have looked at so far, quite reluctant to take credit for the discovery of the female singer's talent or her suc-cess. Hence, having reaffirmed his faith in her singing during their early conversation at her boarding house, he goes on to assert: 'But you know yourself, don't you? You just needed somebody to tell you.' And when her first picture triumphs on opening night (in contrast to the failure of his), he responds in a manner radically different from Cagney's character in *Love Me or Leave Me*. Whereas Marty tried to make Ruth feel indebted for his help in making her a success, Norman does quite the opposite by selflessly encouraging a reluctant Esther to assert her independence from him. 'I've done all I can for you', he tells her at the party; his subsequent words – 'You've come along the road with me as far as you should. Let's leave it that way' – inviting direct contrast with Marty's attempt to emotionally blackmail Ruth by telling her: 'I brought you this far. Nobody else. I did. But that don't count. Not with you. Not with a high-class dame like you.'

However, if *A Star is Born* provides us with the most compelling account so far of the female singer's ability to produce a positive transformation in the male, his belief in her voice provoking a shift in his way of looking at her image that makes him quite untypical of the standard Pygmalion/Svengali male figure, then it also goes much further in depicting his ultimate inability to cope with the strength of her singing voice. Although Norman's insecurity about this becomes increasingly explicit as the narrative progresses, there are signs of it in evidence right from the outset. The moment at the Downbeat Club where he tries to explain to Esther the impact that her singing has had on him is particularly revealing and is worth quoting in full:

Norman:	Do you always sing like that?
Esther:	Like what?
Norman:	The way you sang just now.
Esther:	Why?
Norman:	I never heard anybody sing just the way you do.
Esther:	What do you mean? Good or bad? [She laughs]
Norman:	Here. [He takes her into a back room] Ever go fishing? Well, do you like prizefights? Ever watched a great fighter? [She looks bemused] ... I'm trying to tell you how you sing.
Esther:	Do you mean like a prizefighter or a fish? [She laughs]
Norman:	Look. Here [He takes her into the kitchen] There are certain pleasures that you get. [Then, directing her outside away from the noise] There are certain pleasures you get. Little, little jabs of pleasure, when a ... when a swordfish takes the hook or ... or ... or ... or ... when you watch a great fighter getting ready for the kill, see? You don't understand a word I'm saying, do you?

Esther:	No, not yet. Why don't you try bullfights? [She laughs]
Norman:	You're joking, but that's exactly what I mean. If you'd never seen a bullfight in your life you'd know a great bullfighter the moment he stepped into the ring. From the way he stood, from the way he moved. Or, or a dancer. You don't have to know about ballet. That little bell rings inside your head ... That little jolt of pleasure. Well that's what happened to me just now. You're a great singer.
Esther:	Who, me?
Norman:	Hasn't anyone ever told you that before?
Esther:	No, Mr Maine, no one's ever told me that before. And maybe you're not as sober as we both thought you were. But thank you.
Norman:	I'm as sober as a judge and I know exactly what I'm saying. You've got that little something extra that Ellen Terry talked about. Ellen Terry, great actress long before you were born. She said that's what star quality was ... that little something extra. Well, you've got it.

In resorting to blood-sporting metaphors associated with violence, fighting, ensnarement and killing, Norman thus compliments Esther's singing in a way that conveys an underlying sense of disquiet about its power, the threatening nature of which is here construed as something *intrinsic to the voice itself*, rather than just as a consequence of the female performer's growing material success and professional status. The implied comparison that Norman makes between Esther's performance as a singer and 'a prizefighter going in for the kill' is especially illuminating given the way that it construes this active, forceful assertion of the female voice as tantamount to an intimidating, ruthless display of male power. And while the line about the 'jabs of pleasure' to be felt 'when a swordfish takes the hook' is more ambivalent in the sense that, by equating the male listener with the person fishing, it serves to place Norman in the more dominant role of hunter (thereby reversing Garland's insistence in the song on 'the man' as the one 'that [like the proverbial fish] got away'), the use of terms such as '*sword*fish' and '*jabs* of pleasure' nevertheless suggests a degree of disquiet about the potentially wounding impact of her voice. The phallic nature of the imagery here also hints, more specifically, at the disruptive potential of her voice in gender terms, the destabilising potential of which can be understood in terms of the particular qualities of Garland's voice. With its complex combination of emotional power and vulnerability, bass and treble tonalities, it constitutes, one might say, a kind of refusal of gender stereotyping. This male anxiety about the female singing voice is something that finds further, independent expression in a later scene when Oliver Niles (Charles Bickford), harassed at the prospect of having to close down the production of a movie due to a female performer pulling out of her contract, tells Norman: 'I'm being *stabbed* by a singer in New York' just as Esther's voice (which will replace that of the defaulting performer) can again be heard singing 'The Man That Got Away' from an unidentified source outside the actor's window.

This underlying disquiet about the strength of the female singing voice endows Norman's subsequent gestures of support and appreciation with a much greater ambivalence than what has been suggested s o far. The scene just mentioned where he manages to bring Esther's voice to the attention of Oliver Niles is a case in point. While Norman clearly acts here out of a conscious desire to advance Esther's career, he does so in a way that, by allowing him to stage-manage her singing for Niles' benefit, now ena-bles him to exert a much greater degree of control over her voice than was the case during her first rendition of this song at the Downbeat Club, his position on that occasion being much more that of silent, self-effacing bystander. The moment where Norman asks Esther to sing for him during the honeymoon scene at the Lazybones Motel also becomes infused with a similar ambivalence. Although his request is symptomatic of his willingness, in one sense, to accept her voice as the defining force in their relationship, at the same time it is couched in terms that imply a need to compensate for his self-imposed passivity as listener. Having expressed delight at hearing her number one hit song 'It's a New World' being played on the radio, he switches off this recorded version of her singing and, as if now closing himself off to the influence and status of her voice in the entertainment world at large, proceeds to assert (as if invoking some basic marital right) his wish for her to sing just for him:

> That's for ordinary folks who have to turn on the radio and put a nickel in the jukebox. I've got a private copyright of my own. Including the Scandinavian. I've got the belting original right in the house, every time I want to hear it. And I want it now.

Norman's tendency to intrude into Esther's performing space on two key occasions also acquires a deeper significance when considered in relation to these various indications of his unease about the power of her singing voice. In their effect of disrupting her act and allowing him to take centre stage, such intrusions point both to an unconscious resentment on his part of her vocal dominance and success and to a felt need to reassert his performing superiority over her. In echoing Blackie and Snyder's attempts to intrude into *their* female singer's performing spaces, this trait also provides, in turn, the clearest proof yet of Norman's underlying affinity with his male counterparts in *Love Me or Leave Me* and *San Francisco*, although in his case such behaviour is motivated by much more acute anxieties about the erosion of his own performing identity as an actor. The moment near the beginning of the film where he staggers on stage in a drunken state right in the middle of Esther's number at the Shrine auditorium

provides the first instance of this intrusive pattern of behaviour. Although occurring at a point before Esther has become famous and even before the two characters have properly met, it is an intrusion that nonetheless seems triggered by the threat of seeing his performing identity blanked out (in this case, only temporarily) by the Garland character whose act has been brought on prematurely in place of the temperamental star.

While the disruption posed by this initial intrusion is deftly defused by Esther, who quickly recovers her voice and proceeds to do a comical, improvised dance with Norman, once he is sacked by the studio and starts to feel increasingly threatened by her success this behaviour of his tends to become much more menacing and destructive in its effect. The key scene here is the one at the Oscars ceremony where Norman, having arrived in a drunken state once again and too late to see Esther presented with the 'Best Actress' award, now makes a quite devastating intrusion into her  performing space. His interruption of her 'thank you' speech in order to make a desperate plea for a job has the effect of silencing her voice much more completely on this occasion: 'May I borrow the end of your speech to make a speech of my own?' he asks a distraught Esther. However, he does so in a way that, by providing confirmation to a disenchanted audience of his fall from stardom, only serves to precipitate his downfall even further.

If Norman's drinking tends to trigger moments of aggressive intrusion that, in providing some form of outlet for his male insecurities and resentments, have the effect of temporarily suppressing Esther's voice, then his relapse into alcoholism later on in the film (following his altercation with Libby at the races) ultimately renders him even more vulnerable to her active vocal powers. This is demonstrated most clearly during the scene at the night court when (in a reversal of the scene at the Oscars) she is now shown intruding into his (very different performing) space and then, on hearing him being given a prison sentence (for being drunk and disorderly), pleading with the judge not to send him to jail. As during the scene at the Chicken's Ball in *San Francisco* and the final scene in *Love Me or Leave Me*, then, the male protagonist once again finds himself confronted with a situation where the female singer, acting out of loyalty and indebtedness to her downtrodden lover/husband, seeks to use her voice to help him out of a difficult predicament but in a way that, by highlighting his dependency on her, actually proves to be most oppressive to him. In this case, though, Norman's response is one of helpless anguish rather than active resentment for, on seeing Esther stand up to speak immediately after his sentence is pronounced, he can only silently mouth his wish for her not to intervene. (In this context, it is also worth contrasting Snyder's display of defiant pride when Ruth visits him in jail earlier on in *Love Me or Leave Me* with Norman's much more passive, submissive stance here.) The judge's summing up of his verdict, now revised in the light of Esther's vocal intervention, conveys just how oppressive her influence over Norman has become: 'Sentence suspended. Prisoner remanded to custody of wife.'

The fact that, unlike in those other two films, the woman does not actually need to sing at this point in order to help the male is symptomatic not just of the greater imbalance existing here between her professional status and his disadvantaged state but of *A Star is Born*'s tendency to place greater stress on the ability of the female singer's voice to extend its influence beyond the boundaries of the numbers, often exerting itself in spoken form in ways that become increasingly oppressive to Mason's character. Such tendencies culminate in the following scene at the beachhouse where it is Norman's overhearing of Esther's conversation with Oliver Niles — during which she can be heard revealing her plan to give up her career to be with Norman — that prompts the male protagonist to commit suicide. In a sequence that fulfils the emotionally wounding potential that Norman alluded to in his initial response to hearing Esther sing 'The Man That Got Away' earlier on in the film, it is her voice which, carried on the ocean breeze, intrudes into his bedroom and awakens him from a deep sleep, the intensity and force of feeling embodied in Garland's delivery of the words — 'I love him' — proving to be the very utterance that, in piercing the stillness of his room, first disrupts his repose.

Highly evocative and moving, this sequence derives much of its poetic resonance and poignancy from the rhetorical variations it offers on earlier scenes. Most notable of all is the ironic contrast it invites with the scene immediately after the couple's first encounter at the Shrine auditorium when Norman was on that occasion also shown lying in a deep sleep, the curtains flapping once more in the breeze, only for him to be awoken by his recollection of the number that Esther had just performed on stage with the band. But whereas the music's ability to intrude into his slumbers had served in that instance to suggest the more positive, rejuvenating influence of Esther's singing on Norman, in this case her vocal disruption of his sleeping state proves to have quite the reverse effect. Although he appears in the next scene apparently refreshed and ready to turn over a new leaf, his rejuvenation turns out to be only an act put on for Esther's benefit, his apparent eagerness to go for a swim masking his real wish to commit suicide.

This sequence where Norman overhears Esther talking to Oliver Niles also offers an ironic reworking of that other earlier scene where Norman contrived it so that the studio head would hear a recording of Esther's singing outside the actor's dressing room. Although both scenes are again linked by this basic scenario involving Esther's voice intruding into a room and capturing the attention of an unsuspecting male listener, in the later scene Norman is clearly not in a position to control her voice in the way that he was before. His active stage-managing of the earlier situation by opening the window so as to enable Niles to overhear Esther's singing thus finds its inverse scenario here as Norman lies passively and help-lessly in bed, her voice now exerting a most dreadful hold over him as he listens, weighed down by the terrible implications of what she says, his own stifled sobbing (as he turns his face into the pillow) in contrast going quite unheard by her or Niles.

Esther: You're very fond of
            him, aren't you
            Oliver?
Oliver: I'm very fond of
            both of you.
Esther: Then I know you'll
            understand what I have to tell you. You probably
            know already after what happened last night. I
            can't do any more pictures, Oliver. I'm going away
            for good. With Norman.
Oliver: You're at the very height of your career, Esther.
            The very peak of your success.
Esther: There wouldn't be any career without Norman. I'm
            just giving back the gift he gave me.
Oliver: No one can give anyone a career. You've made
            your own.
Esther: No! No! He gave it to me, by his faith and by his
            love. And without him, it's just nothing. Not the
            way things are.

In showing Norman so totally weighed down by the burden of Esther's indebtedness to him (an indebtedness which in this case prompts the female singer not to sing on his behalf but to give up her career instead), this sequence provides the most deeply revealing insight yet into the oppressiveness of the Pygmalion/Svengali role for the male himself. What Norman is forced to confront here, in effect, as he lies listening to Esther's emotional declaration of her indebtedness to him, are the destructive consequences arising from the female singer's own internalisation of the assumption (more typically voiced by the male himself in moments of crisis when his control over the female is under threat) that she owes everything to him – or, to put it again in the context of the Pygmalion myth, that he 'made' her what she is in professional terms. Norman's status as a much more troubled, tragically self-aware male mentor figure (compared to his counterparts in *San Francisco* and *Love Me or Leave Me*) endows Esther's words here with a doubly oppressive impact. In hearing her announce her decision to give up her career for his sake, he becomes burdened not only by the prospect of destroying her career (as he had earlier feared) but also by the consequent threat of himself becoming even more unbearably indebted to her than before. And while Oliver Niles offers some resistance to Esther's reading of her situation ('No one can give anyone a career. You've made your own.') he does so in a manner that only serves to reinforce Norman's insecurities even further:

> Esther, I have to tell you this. I hate to but I must. There's nothing left anymore. It happened long before last night. Long before we let him out of the studio. Twenty years of steady and quiet drinking do something to a man. Long before it showed in his face, it showed in his acting. Little by little, more and more, with each picture. That's why he slipped. It wasn't just bad pictures, it was him. And there's nothing left anymore. He's just a shell of what he once was. It's gone, Esther.

Although Oliver's frank assessment of the decline in Norman's acting ability is partly belied by the latter's moving performance as the rejuvenated, reformed male in the very next scene, in playing this part, Norman engages in a form of knowing pretence that (unlike its equivalent playacting scenario in *The Pirate*) can only afford him release through oblivion and death. The fact that Norman asks Esther to sing for him as he makes his way down to the beach to commit suicide further problematises the nature of the release available to him here as his use of her singing to steel himself to the task ahead implies a dependency on the female singer's voice even at the very point where he seeks to free himself from his mounting obligation to her. And although Esther's reprisal of the song 'It's a New World' is clearly intended by her as a reaffirmation of both her love for him and her ongoing indebtedness to him ('You brought a new world to me. And that it'll always, always be.') in choosing the song that marked her rise to movie stardom she unwittingly provides Norman with a musical reminder of the precise moment when her success first began to eclipse his.

The overwhelming effect of Esther's singing on Norman is conveyed most of all, though, through the properties of the female voice itself which here becomes endowed with an almost omnipresent quality as, carried once again on the ocean breeze, it follows and surrounds him as he makes his way down to the shoreline. Indeed if, as Michel Chion suggests, 'Water and the voice are two instances of that which has neither location nor border  unless we assign them one' (1999: 113), then this particular sequence would seem to invite a rather compelling link to be made between the fluid, floating qualities of the female singer's voice and the formless, uncontainable properties of the sea.[5] This rhetorical link between voice and sea (especially compelling given the latter's traditional associations with femininity) consequently endows Norman's suicide with a further significance. For if the ocean can be construed as a kind of visual extension of Esther's singing voice, then his act of drowning tends to literalise his sense of being engulfed by her vocal power, the act of walking into the sea suggesting a final, voluntary subsuming of his identity into hers.

The ability of the female singer's voice to generate and articulate a whole range of gender-related anxieties and concerns centred on the theme of identity culminates in the final scene when, having decided to go ahead with her performance at the Shrine auditorium despite her grief over Norman's death, Esther appears on stage and introduces herself in the following highly emotional terms: 'Hello, everybody. This is Mrs ... Norman ... Maine.' Extremely resonant in terms of what has gone before, this moment also offers a more extreme version of the tensions and tendencies inherent in *Love Me or Leave Me*'s final scene. As in that film, the female singer is shown going on stage with the intention of acknowledging her debt of gratitude to the male protagonist whose influence continues to exert itself within the scene. But whereas the male's continuing influence over the female singer was registered in *Love Me or Leave Me* quite independently of the woman herself (via the inclusion in the decor of the 'MS' emblem embroidered in the curtain drape hanging above her), in this case it is actually embodied in Esther's own vocal tribute, the content of which clearly signals the extent to which she is now defining her sense of identity in relation to his. And whereas Ruth's appearance on stage in Marty's club is construed very much as a pragmatic repayment of an old debt and one that promises to rid the female singer of her obligation to the male once and for all, in Esther's case her appearance on stage constitutes a defiant demonstration of her ongoing commitment to Norman whose suicide has only served to make her even more indebted to him than before. Although Esther's feelings of indebtedness to Norman now seem to compel her to continue with her career, rather than give it up, the film ends not (as in *Love Me or Leave Me*) with a celebration of the woman's *singing* but with the female using her *speaking* voice to pay tribute to the male. Indeed, it is even possible to find, in Esther's verbal acknowledgement of Norman Maine here, a more subtle version of this male protagonist's earlier intrusions into her performing space. For if in the opening scene Norman was able to overcome his initial absence through drunkenness by going on stage in the middle of Esther's act, then on this occasion his 'appearance'

in her vocal tribute still has the effect (in prompting a standing ovation from the audience) of holding up her act and stalling her from singing.

So while both films end with the female singer using her voice to redefine her sense of identity in the light of her involvement with an influential male mentor figure, in Esther's case, the extent of the negotiation that takes place is much more extreme. Having initially construed her voice as a vital means by which to express her selfhood ('But I had to sing. Somehow I feel most alive when I'm singing', she told Norman near the beginning of the film), she now uses it to signal a voluntary subsuming of her identity into his. But any such relinquishment of independence on Esther's part is complicated immeasurably by the fact that it is motivated by a most moving commitment (born out of profound feelings of love rather than mere gratitude) to saving Norman's own identity from oblivion. This was made clear during the previous scene when her unwillingness to appear at the benefit was overcome by the warning given to her by Danny (Tommy Noonan): 'You're the only thing that remains of him now. And if you just kick it away, it's like he never existed. Like there never was a Norman Maine at all.' In circumstances again much more extreme than those in play at the end of *Love Me or Leave Me*, the female singer's voice becomes the one thing capable of sustaining the male's identity by the narrative close. Such a situation on this occasion requires the female to take the far more drastic action of using her voice to absorb his identity into hers. In doing so, Esther completes the process of assimilation and merging that began during the couple's first encounter at the Shrine auditorium when, having gone on stage to cover up another of Norman's non-appearances, she responded to his subsequent intrusion during her number by incorporating his body into her performance act.

In view of the fact that *A Star is Born* marked Garland's comeback as a Hollywood actress following MGM's termination of her contract in 1950 and was released by Warner Bros. at a time when the difficulties experienced by this star in her personal life (including rumours of at least one suicide attempt) were becoming more publicly known (see Dyer 1986: 142–3, 150–2), this subsuming of Norman's identity into Esther's clearly acquires a further level of significance. It is a meaning that was encouraged during the couple's very first encounter, in fact, for, in that moment when Norman comes staggering onto the stage in the middle of Esther's act at the Shrine auditorium, it is almost as if, in star terms, Garland is being confronted with an image of her own more unstable off-screen persona, an alter ego figure whose unwelcome intrusion has to be faced up to and overcome in order to enable the performance to go ahead. The possibility of reading Norman Maine as an embodiment of Garland's off-screen star persona is something that the film also encourages elsewhere through the use of various mirroring strategies. A quite literal example of this occurs in the

very next scene to the one just mentioned when, as Esther is shown bend-
ing down in front of a mirror to apply some lipstick while commenting to
Danny on Norman's temperamental star behaviour ('It's a wonder to me
that Mr Norman Maine is still in pictures' she remarks), Mason's character
suddenly appears from behind, his reflection clearly visible in the mirror
in front of her.

Given such extra- and intra-textual links between Garland and Mason's
character, Esther's introduction of herself as 'Mrs Norman Maine' at the
end can therefore be read as both articulating and bringing to a close
this further complex play on the relationship between voice, image and
identity in *A Star is Born*. Indeed, if the rest of the film can be understood
in terms of this multi-layered performance scenario whereby James Mason
plays an actor who is not just 'his character' but an extension or projec-
tion of his co-star's off-screen persona, then this would seem to find its
ultimate acknowledgement and resolution in Garland's (not just Esther's)
ominous verbal embracing of Norman Maine's identity at the end.

What's Love Got To Do With It

On turning to *What's Love Got To Do With It* (Brian Gibson, 1993), it is possible to find in this more contemporary musical biopic about the life and
career of the singer Tina Turner a further significant development in this
fascination with the great female singer. The first basic difference to note
is that unlike the other musical biopics we have looked at so far, where
the performer whose life story is the subject of the narrative is played by
an established, successful female singer in her own right, in this case Tina
Turner (real name Anna Mae Bullock) is played by the non-singing female
star Angela Bassett whose voice is dubbed by Turner's throughout each of
the musical numbers. That this use of a non-singing star does not weaken
the overall premise of the film is due largely to the compelling way in
which Bassett inhabits her role on screen. Her ability to render the character's emotional life with such depth and conviction allied with her adept-
ness in capturing the intense physicality of Tina Turner's performances on
stage all help to facilitate our acceptance of this dramatic conjoining of
singer's voice and actress's body.

The handling of the very first moment where such a union occurs is
also crucial in lending further conviction to this scenario whereby Angela

Bassett borrows Tina Turner's singing voice during the musical numbers in exchange for the actress lending out her body to the singer for the duration of the narrative. The sequence in question occurs fairly early on in the film when Anna Mae is shown obtaining her first opportunity to sing with Ike (Laurence Fishburne) and his band during one of the regular audience participation sessions at the Club Royal. What is so notable here is the way that, as Angela Bassett takes the microphone and begins to move towards the stage, the camera shifts to a vantagepoint somewhere among the crowd (looking up at Ike on stage) just as the singer's rendition of the song '(Darlin') You Know I Love You' strikes up on the soundtrack. In adopting this audience viewpoint at the very moment when Tina Turner's singing is heard for the first time, the film creates the impression of her voice emerging from somewhere akin to our own spectatorial space within the cinema auditorium. This, coupled with the fact that, for the duration of this particular shot, we can hear Tina Turner's voice but cannot yet actually see Bassett performing as the singer helps to create the momentary sensation that this disembodied voice could, in fact, be our own as, sitting in the auditorium, we project our fantasies onto the screen. The subsequent cut to a shot showing Anna Mae now singing has the effect of attaching the singer's voice more securely to the body of Bassett, our alignment with whom is strengthened considerably by the way that her character begins (like us) as an ordinary spectator in the crowd before then making the transition to high-octane performer on stage. Such a sequence, poised at the all-important moment of discovery, perfectly exemplifies the liberating, empowering potential of the great female singer's voice as, first directly and then via our narrative stand-in, we temporarily gain access to a level and form of expression unavailable to us within our ordinary lives.

In terms of its impact on the male protagonist, however, this release of female vocal energy is something that (as in many of the other films we have looked at) tends to provoke a more ambivalent response. This is made clear during the very next scene at the restaurant when Ike can be heard describing the effect of Anna Mae's singing in a way that conveys both the fascination and threat that her voice holds for him:

> Mmm-mm-mm. Anna Mae! Girl, you shocked the hell out of me. Where'd a little woman like you get such a big voice? You had them folks tore down in there, like ... let me put it to you this way. See,

it's like you sang like a man. I mean you are a woman. You are a
woman. Any man can see that, but, girl, it's like you got your own
particular way of gettin' a song outta ya. It's unique. You got your
own unique sound.

If Ike's assertion that Anna Mae 'sang like a man' invites comparison
with Norman Maine's use of very 'masculine' blood-sporting metaphors
to describe the impact of Esther's singing on him during the scene at
the Downbeat Club in *A Star is Born*, then overall *What's Love...* is much
bleaker in its study of the male's increasingly violent responses to the
woman's growing autonomy and status as a singer. His inability to master
her *voice* (despite Ike's more explicit attempts to manipulate it during
certain recording sessions) in this film gives rise to increasingly brutal
assaults on her *body*. This culminates in the sequence where, having
witnessed the success of Anna Mae's first solo recording hit 'River Deep,
Mountain High' and their fans' growing adulation of her, a drugged-up Ike
is shown ranting at her for not singing the lyrics to 'Nutbush City' the way
he insists he told her to before then proceeding to rape her in his recording studio. It is a response on the part of the male that, displaying none
of Norman Maine's respect for the female singer's image and none of the
regard for her talent that led that figure to turn his destructive tendencies
inwardly on himself, on this occasion compels the woman herself to contemplate suicide as a release from her despair.

The use of the recording studio as the setting for the rape reinforces
the utter desolation of this moment. Instead of providing the female, as
in *Love Me or Leave Me*, with a protective, creative musical space where,
free from the husband's possessive control, she could begin to reassert
the autonomy of her singing voice and thereby in the process rediscover a
more meaningful sense of selfhood, in *What's Love...* the recording studio
becomes an entrapping, all too easily violated space where the woman's
voice and identity are negated in the most dehumanising way possible.
The ability of *What's Love...* to go much further in exposing the violent consequences arising from the male's attempts to control the female singer
can be understood partly, of course, in terms of the very different production conditions that were in place in the 1990s compared to the 1950s
when stricter censorship rules were in force. Indeed, it is worth noting, in
this regard, that the scene in *Love Me or Leave Me* where Snyder tries to

force himself on Etting was itself originally filmed as a rape only to be then substantially cut by the censors (see Braun 2004: 144).

Yet if the changed production conditions (and overall cultural climate) of the 1990s allowed *What's Love...* greater freedom in tackling these disturbing aspects to Tina Turner's life story (which was, of course, already so well known to the public), then they surely also enabled it to go much further in its celebration of the singer's rebellion against such oppression and her subsequent recreation of herself as an independent performing identity in her own right. In making the African American female the subject of this journey towards emancipation and self-discovery, *What's Love...* also develops many of the progressive tendencies that we found (in chapter 1) to be at work in *Cabin in the Sky*, effectively following through, in much freer fashion, what that earlier film had sought to do within the far more challenging confines of the all-black musical form. The affinities that these two films share in this regard is evident in a number of ways, perhaps finding most vivid expression in a series of detailed rhyming moments and scenes. In both films, for example, the African American female's need to break free from the traditional constraints of her rural world is encapsulated in those moments where she is shown straying from the religious forms of music expected of her in favour of a more contemporary urban black sound. In *Cabin in the Sky*, this takes the form of Petunia's gravitation towards an increasingly jazz-like style of singing during the 'Taking a Chance on Love' number while in *What's Love...* it manifests itself in the rhythm 'n' blues influences that the young Anna Mae (Rae Ven Kelly) instinctively injects into the gospel song she sings at church as a child. In both cases, these displays of musical deviancy are quickly suppressed – in *Cabin in the Sky*, by Joe's abrupt termination of Petunia's growling outburst at the end of her number, in *What's Love...* by the female chorister's stern reprimand of Anna Mae and, when this does not work, by her eviction of the child from the church.

However, in each film the female protagonist's ensuing journey into the urban sphere of the nightclub seems to offer her the possibility of a more liberating space where she can escape the limitations of her former world and discover, through the contemporary rhythms of the music that is played there, a freer, more meaningful form of self-expression. The scene depicting Anna Mae's second visit to the club where Ike and his band play invites particularly strong parallels with the one where Petunia visits Jim

Henry's Paradise Club. Like her predecessor in *Cabin in the Sky*, Anna Mae is shown causing quite a stir by appearing in a glamorous dress that signals her intention to cast off her naïve, rural black persona in favour of an identity associated with a more independent, active form of female sexuality, the assertion of which is again given fuller vent through the woman's launching into a song. In the case of *What's Love...*, though, this movement into the nightclub sphere is indicative of the black female protagonist's ability to effect a much more complete break away from her former rural environment, following on, as it does, from the sequence depicting the adult Anna Mae's journey by bus to the actual city of St Louis. This geographical shift, occurring directly after the brief introductory sequence dealing with the young Anna Mae's far from idealised childhood in the rural south, also demonstrates the film's own capacity to distance itself from the spatial and ideological restrictions of the all-black musical form. This is further suggested by its use of subtitles both here and elsewhere to signal the precise location and year of certain key events. All of these serve – together with the adoption of other documentary-style techniques (including reconstructions of interviews and broadcasted performances given by Ike and Tina Turner) – to ground the narrative in a more concrete sense of time and place.

What's Love...'s ability to go further than *Cabin in the Sky* in its exploration of the experiential journey undertaken by the black female protagonist extends to its treatment of the entrapping, not just liberating, consequences arising from her movement into the urban world. While both films seek to problematise the woman's attempt to gain release from her former position by showing her quickly becoming involved with a male figure who, having initially appeared to embody the liberating potential of the nightclub world, ultimately ends up exerting a sexually oppressive hold over her, in *What's Love...* the problematic nature of such a relationship becomes a far more central, driving concern of the narrative. Ultimately, though, *What's Love...*'s uncompromising approach to its subject matter does enable it to move towards a much more emphatic celebration of the woman's rebellion against such oppression. Thus, whereas the ideological pressures inherent in the all-black musical form eventually forced *Cabin in the Sky* to conclude its highly subversive nightclub sequence by showing Petunia lapsing back (albeit ironically) into a passive reliance on her former Christian faith, *What's Love...* instead stresses the self-empowering potential of an alternative religion like Buddhism in enabling Anna Mae to break free altogether from the oppressiveness of her situation.[6] At one point during her comeback as a solo artist, she can be heard explaining the significance of this religion to her in a television interview:

> In Buddhism we do a chant called 'Nam myoho renge kyo' and what that signifies is that everything in our life is cause and effect. If there's anything within you that needs to be changed, you do it. You change it...

As the character who first introduces Anna Mae to Buddhism, Jackie (Vanessa Bell Calloway) acts as a refreshingly positive black female alternative to the controlling male mentor figure in the Hollywood musical. By encouraging her friend to take up chanting, she allows the singer to find an outlet for her voice that is free from Ike's obsessive control, this rediscovery of some sense of vocal autonomy once again proving crucial (as in the other films we have studied) to the woman's ability to redefine her sense of selfhood. Anna Mae's visit to Jackie's house (following the singer's recovery from her suicide attempt) consequently becomes a pivotal turning point in the narrative. The importance of this scene is compounded by the way that Anna Mae's introduction to Buddhist chanting is preceded by a transformative moment of role play wherein the two women each take turns in pretending to be Ike. It is a highly self-conscious, ironic piece of acting on the two women's part that, in enabling them to mock the performative nature of Ike's aggressive male posturing and the kind of role play that he expects of Anna Mae both on- and off-stage, seems to allow the female protagonist to gain a more distanced, outsider perspective on her marriage. And it is on witnessing her friend acting out a parodic version of both marital roles by herself at one point – in an exchange that involves Jackie playing the part first of the abusive, tyrannical Ike, then of a deferential, timid Tina, and then of Ike again – that finally brings Anna Mae to the point where, no longer able to continue with her own part in this mock performance, she drops the mask and, breaking down in tears, expresses her feelings of despair.

As in *The Pirate*, then, it is a self-conscious, ironic acting out of entrapping sex roles that again proves instrumental in facilitating an escape from gender oppression, providing a moment that paves the way for a more liberating, self-affirming form of musical performance in the final number. And as in that earlier musical, this sense of gaining release is heightened by the suggestion of a further stripping away of performance layers during the course of the final number itself. In what is a striking reworking of that moment right at the very end of the 'Be a Clown' number where Gene Kelly and Judy Garland appear to let go of their character masks and be

themselves (as they laugh uncontrollably at the performance they have just given (see Dyer 1986: 186)), the film suddenly cuts, mid-way through its final number, from a sequence showing Angela Bassett performing on stage *as* Tina Turner to one showing Turner performing the same song *herself* in concert. In an even more precise echo of that final moment in *The Pirate*, we are then privileged with a much more intimate view of Tina Turner as the singer at one point faces the camera directly and smiles gleefully while performing a brief jaunty little dance on stage. Following a full-length view of her completing this nimble piece of

footwork, the film proceeds to frame her face in close-up as she first beams warmly at the camera before then throwing her head back and laughing exuberantly in a manner that seems to signal her sense of delight at the freedom of performance she now enjoys.

Yet while the utopian sensibility of these two films appears very alike in this sense, where *What's Love...* differs quite significantly from its predecessor is in its ability to contemplate a notion of gender freedom that neither involves the kind of collapse of sexual difference that seemed to occur in that earlier film's final number nor requires the woman's achievement to be subsumed into a wider celebration of the couple. The film's final number does raise the question, though, of whether such independence is bought at the expense of a rejection of love altogether, with the main title line – 'What's love got to do with it?' – contrasting quite noticeably with the notion of 'Taking a Chance on Love' that is celebrated in the song reprised by Ethel Waters at the end of *Cabin in the Sky*. Elsewhere, too, the lyrics display a further scepticism about the value of love itself ('What's love but a second-hand emotion?), together with a wariness about the dangers of emotional commitment ('Who needs a heart when a heart can be broken?') and a need to deny that relationships are based on anything more than purely physical attraction ('You must try to ignore that it means more than that').

But if the decision to base both the title and ending of the film on this number could be criticised for distorting the original emphasis of the singer's biography (in the book *I, Tina,* this song by the male composer/ musician Terry Britten figures as only one of several elements covered in the account of the singer's comeback success) then when considered in relation to the conventions of the backstage musical as a whole, the lyrics of 'What's Love Got To Do With It?' acquire a more appropriately rebellious charge. Indeed, if the backstage musical has often stressed the inter-relationship between career and romance where the woman is concerned (in a musical like *White Christmas* (Michael Curtiz, 1954) this even extends to the assumption that the female singer will automatically give up her place in the 'Sisters' act once the prospect of marriage arises)[7] then *What's Love...*'s much reiterated title refrain can be read as a kind of insistent challenging of this generic premise that romance will always have something to do with the female's performing destiny: 'What's love go to do, got to do with it?'

In offering such an emphatic celebration of the woman's emancipa- tion, *What's Love...*'s ending also marks a significant development in the musical's ongoing fascination with the great female singer. Radically different in tone from Esther's moving affirmation of her love for Norman Maine at the end of *A Star is Born* (a love that can only be expressed, however, through the woman's voluntary merging of her identity with his), *What's Love...*'s final sequence seems closer in the overall tenor of its narrative resolution to *Love Me or Leave Me*. However, unlike Etting, the Angela Bassett character is already well free of her obligation to the male protagonist by the start of the film's final number. *What's Love...* provides just one lingering reminder of Ike's former control over the female singer's performing identity when, in a visual echo of the wreath bearing the ini- tials 'M.S.' that hangs above the Doris Day character as she performs at Marty's nightclub, the first part of the stage name that Ike gave to Anna

Mae is displayed prominently above Tina Turner's head in the second half of the final number. But, unlike its counterpart in *Love Me or Leave Me* and in contrast to Esther's verbal embracing of Norman Maine's identity at the end of *A Star is Born*, it is the female part of the name – 'TINA' – which, shorn of its marital, patriarchal associations, is foregrounded here (as it is in the title of the singer's written biography). Added to that, the over-whelming feeling created by the number is of the female's success in refashioning this male-constructed name into an identifiable performing identity of her own. This notion was established much earlier in the film, in fact, most notably, after one of the couple's concert performances when the audience can be heard chanting the name 'Tina' while the overlooked Ike stands in the background, clearly resentful of the extent to which her performances have taken on a life and identity of their own. It is also strongly asserted during the scene at the divorce court when Anna Mae is shown winning her right to use the name 'Tina Turner' in a way that is now no longer dependent on her marriage to Ike.

This sense of the female singer being able to refashion her perform-ing identity in a way that is now free of the male protagonist's control is emphatically reinforced by the transition that takes place mid-way during the final number from the sequence depicting Angela Bassett performing as Tina Turner within the narrative to one showing Tina Turner herself on stage at one of her real-life concert venues. In creating (in that second half of the number) an autonomous, impervious performing space out-side of the story diegesis into which Ike cannot intrude, *What's Love...* effectively brings to a halt that ongoing pattern of male invasion into the woman's performing space that has been such a prominent feature in the biopic/backstage musicals covered in this chapter and which in this film manifested itself just moments before the start of the final number. On that occasion, Ike was shown entering Anna Mae's dressing room (having bypassed security) and trying to stop her from going on-stage by threaten-ing her with a gun before then hovering at the back of the auditorium as she performs her song to an adoring audience. This aggressive act of intru-sion, initially thwarted by Anna Mae's defiant refusal to be put off by his threat of violence, is then followed by the film's own much more complete expulsion of this controlling male figure from the woman's performing space. The precise timing of Fishburne's disappearance – as he is shown walking down a darkened alley right at the end of the Angela Bassett section of the number – is particularly effective in highlighting (along with the accompanying subtitle informing us of Ike's subsequent conviction and imprisonment on drug-related charges) this symbolic breaking of all ties with the male protagonist.

As well as providing the female singer with a performing space free from male intrusion and control, this shift from Bassett to Turner also has the effect of returning the woman's singing voice to its original bodily source, thereby achieving a union of voice and image that plays centrally into the idea of a stronger, more independent performing identity asserting itself at the end. This process of restoring the female singing voice to its rightful owner by the end of the film is something that we also traced in *Singin' in the Rain* earlier on in this chapter. However, whereas the voice acted in that film as a source of conflict and betrayal for the two female characters *within* the narrative, with the resolution to such tensions only being achieved at the end through the chastisement of the actress (Lina Lamont) who had previously benefited from the dubbing of the other woman's singing, in this case the borrowing and return of the woman's voice tends to evoke a much more positive sense of black female solidarity between actress and singer. That is not to say that this shift in performance register is entirely free from disruption as the use of subtitles triumphantly proclaiming the commercial, world-wide success of Tina Turner during the opening two shots of her on stage does feel just a little intrusive while the sudden transition from actress to singer also has the effect of foregrounding the differences in physical appearance of the two women (particularly the more highly developed muscularity of Bassett's body compared to Tina Turner's). But amidst all this, it is the voice which, acting as an aural bridge that spans both halves of the number, helps bind the two women's individual performances on stage into a more harmonious, collective whole. It does so in a way that – rather than undermining or betraying the integrity of Bassett's overall performance – encourages us to read the actress's moving portrayal of Tina Turner's life within the narrative and the singer's actual experience in the world outside as part of an overall continuum.

In using Tina Turner's voice to articulate utopian feelings of female empowerment, female freedom and black female solidarity at the end, *What's Love...* also manages to refute what could, conceivably, be put forward as one possible counter-argument about these films. Namely that, in focusing on the female singer's troubled personal life, they effectively carry out an elaborate strategy of containment of their own, the extensive narrative emphasis on the woman's traumatisation by the male thereby functioning, in this sense, as a method for defusing the potency of her voice within the musical passages. However, as we have seen with regard to *What's Love...*'s ending, this is countered by the way that (having offered a sustained interrogation of the problematic masculinities at work within the backstage world of the musical) the narratives ultimately progress towards some form of moving affirmation or celebration of the resilience[8] and regenerative powers of the female singer's voice as she seeks to redefine her identity in the light of her involvement with some influential male mentor figure. Indeed, as well as offering complex individual meditations on the nature of gender identity and heterosexual relationships in the backstage musical, the last three films covered in this chapter can also be understood as forming part of a broader development of such concerns, with the endings, viewed inter-textually, producing an overall trajectory of release that culminates in the female singer finally asserting her autonomy as a performing self in her own right.

3   CONCLUSION

Throughout this study, it has been argued that while the musical's utopian vision has often been expressed in ways that seem designed to serve the dominant needs of white patriarchal society, there are areas of the Hollywood musical that demonstrate a much more progressive attitude towards race and gender, the full complexities of which have tended to be obscured by some of the broader, theoretical approaches that have been applied to the genre. In acknowledging the existence of both such tendencies, it is accepted that this study to some extent bears out Richard Dyer's notion that the musical is a form characterised by ideological contradiction and struggle. Writing about this in relation to show business more broadly, Dyer argues in the opening section to his seminal essay 'Entertainment and Utopia' that:

> The fact that professional entertainment has been by and large conservative in this century should not blind us to the implicit struggle within it, and looking beyond class to divisions of sex and race, we should note the important role of structurally subordinate groups in society – women, blacks, gays – in the development and definition of entertainment. In other words, show business's relationship to the demands of patriarchal capitalism is a complex one. Just as it does not simply 'give the people what they want' (since it actually defines those wants), so, as a relatively autonomous mode of cultural production, it does not simply reproduce unproblematically patriarchal-capitalist ideology. Indeed, it is pre-

cisely on seeming to achieve both these often opposed functions simultaneously that its survival largely depends. (1981: 177)

Yet while Dyer tends to see this contradiction as operating in a way that 'effectively denies the legitimacy of other needs and inadequacies, and especially of class, patriarchal and sexual struggles' ('that is, while entertainment is responding to needs that are real, at the same time it is defining and delimiting what constitute the legitimate needs of people in this society') (1981: 184), this study has focused on an area of the musical that, as well as showing a sensitivity to the creative possibilities arising from the use of black and female performers (in particular), has also demonstrated a readiness to confront and explore (at times quite *coherently*) the realities of racial and gender oppression. Not only that but, in analysing a number of major musicals that demonstrate such characteristics, the study has also revealed some notable instances of where individual films have managed to problematise and disturb some of the racial and gender assumptions underpinning the conventions of the genre itself. In the examples that we have covered, the extent of the challenge that these texts pose in this respect is evidenced by the considerable strain that such strategies and concerns place on their status as musicals, as they seek to resist what Dyer regards as the musical's more dominant tendency of trying to work through and efface the gap between social needs and inadequacies on the one hand and utopian solutions on the other.

In chapter 1, this more generically self-critical approach took the form of an implied questioning of the white-determined nature of the musical's utopian vision, while in chapter 2 it manifested itself in a quite extensive interrogation of the structures of male domination underpinning the world of the backstage musical and (linked to this) the Pygmalion/Galatea, Svengali/Trilby power relations that tend to influence the formulation of heterosexual relationships in this and other areas of the musical. In exploring how these complex meanings and effects are achieved, the study has demonstrated the importance of paying attention both to the detailed fabric of the musical text and the intricate web of patterns that link certain groups of texts. In the case of performance alone, we explored a whole range of areas, with the tensions that arise within and between individual performances, the interactions that occur between performance and aspects such as music and spatial setting, the relationship between image and song, the positioning of numbers within the narratives, the impact of performance on the narratives, and the creative dialectics established between different registers of performance (both musical and non-musical) all proving crucial to the analysis. In addressing how the overall interplay of textual and inter-textual elements contributes to the achievements of the films in question, it is hoped that the study has, in turn, helped to reveal a more thoughtful side to the musical than the latter is generally given credit for. In demonstrating how the fluid, intangible qualities of the singing voice provide opportunities for the expression of a more distinctive form of identity that is capable of resisting stereotypical notions of race and gender, it is also hoped that this study has gone some way towards suggesting the limitations of a dominantly image-centred approach to the musical, the priorities of which have often tended to obfuscate this crucial dimension to the genre. Indeed, what is so interesting about the musicals covered in chapter 2 is the way in which they explicitly challenge the supposed primacy of the image by foregrounding the importance of the voice as a more important marker of identity for the woman than her body. In the case of the backstage musicals about the great female singer, they proved particularly effective in using this figure's stronger, more charismatic voice to destabilise traditional male ways of controlling (and looking at) women. In using the great female singer to bring about a significant re-definition of the relationship between voice, image and identity, these films therefore do much to suggest the need to rethink the terms of our own academic, critical agenda.

NOTES

1   Rogin maintains that such cultural exclusion is compounded by the way that the film, in line with dominant trends in white mainstream entertainment at that time, appropriates the distinctly urban music of the modern, cosmopolitan Negro, in this case diluting it and filtering it through the caricatured mask and nostalgic rural myth of blackness.

2   In the CD liner notes to John McGlinn's reconstructed recording of the music that was originally designed for the 1928 stage production of *Show Boat*, Miles Kreuger (who has carried out some archival research on the show's history) takes a rather different view of the lyrics to 'Old Man River'. For him, 'Hammerstein's 'use of the word "nigger" is not a white writer's attempt to be derogatory or flippant, but rather an una-shamed expression of artistic honesty' (1988: 23). He goes on to argue that 'in the case of *Show Boat*, the use of "niggers" as the very opening word serves stunningly to shock an audience from its complacency, to consider (at least subconsciously) the servile conditions to which southern Negroes were subjected a century ago. The word is therefore an indictment against those times and conditions, not against the Negro race' (ibid.). So whereas Dyer reads the changes to this song in the 1936 version of *Show Boat* in terms of Robeson's more radical star qualities, Kreuger considers it as part of a broader, more politically cor-rect attempt to sanitise the play of its original gritty power: 'First it was "*Niggers* all work on de Mississippi"; in the 1936 film it was "*Darkies*

all work on de Mississippi" [sic]; in the 1946 revival it was "*Colored folks* work on de Mississippi"; in *Till The Clouds Roll By* it was "*Here we all* work on de Mississippi"; and by the 1966 revival *nobody* worked on the Mississippi, because the opening Negro chorus was omitted altogether' (ibid.).

3   In her article on *Blonde Venus* (Josef von Sternberg, 1932), Deborah Thomas also cites *Cabin in the Sky* when referring to the existence of more progressive treatments of race in American cinema (see Thomas 1990: 7).

4   Naremore also remarks on how 'the "Hotel Hades" … resembles the office of an MGM producer during a story conference' (1993: 66).

5   In arguing for the racial and gender related significance of Joe's gift of the electric washing machine, I would tend to disagree with Naremore who construes the inclusion of this object as an example of how Minnelli's 'dreamy settings' 'tended to aestheticise poverty' in ways that produced 'some condescending jokes'. For him, 'the washer becomes a surrealistic image … which both satirises and validates the society of consumption' (1993: 66).

6   Naremore refers very briefly to how the 'Taking a Chance on Love' number 'uses the metaphor of gambling (Joe's major vice) to speak about monogamous romance' (1993: 64) but he does not dwell on the more subversive implications arising from this. Petunia's visit to the nightclub is also referred to in similarly brief terms (1993: 68).

7   Jacqui Malone describes improvisation as 'an additive process … a way of experimenting with new ideas' and one that manifests itself in 'the tendency toward elasticity of form in African American art' (1996: 33).

8   According to Malone, as African American dance evolved it developed a 'uniquely American' style of dancing, one that, in its emphasis upon 'bent knees and angulated bodies', was 'in striking contrast to the erect spines, straight legs, turned-out feet, and rounded arms of the European American dancing instructors' that slaves and freed blacks encountered during festivals in the South and North (1996: 49).

Chapter Two

1   In her discussion of Streisand's Jewishness in 'Hardly Chazans: *Yentl* and the Singing Jew', Michele Aaron notes how this star's role as Fanny

Brice in some ways exemplifies the kind of 'ugly duckling' stereotype that Patricia Erens sees as belonging to 'cinema's derogatory portraits of Jews'. However, Aaron also points out that 'a recurrent theme in Streisand's films is that of triumphing – becoming a swan – despite the odds' (2000: 126).

2   According to various accounts of the film's production history, the studio first considered using Hepburn's singing but then decided that it was too limited to cope with the vocal range demanded by most of the songs. Regarding Hepburn's obliviousness to the fact that her voice was being dubbed, Alexander Walker explains (in the BBC Omnibus documentary *My Fair Lady: 'Wouldn't it be Loverly'* (2001)) that: 'She didn't know that while she was acting the role and George Cukor was directing her, Marni Nixon was secretly recording the songs so that they could be dubbed over Audrey's lip movements.'

3   Interestingly, in the DVD release version of the film one of the special features allows one to listen to Hepburn's own original recordings of the two numbers 'Wouldn't It Be Loverly?' and 'Show Me'.

4   According to most accounts that I have read, Debbie Reynolds' voice was itself dubbed on three occasions: first by Betty Royce during the sequence where Kathy is shown singing the words of the song 'Would You?' for Lina Lamont (during the making of the film 'The Dancing Cavalier'); then by Jean Hagen herself during the sequence where Kathy is shown recording a section of Lina's dialogue for that same film; and then again by Betty Royce during Reynolds' final duet with Gene Kelly in the number 'You Are My Lucky Star'. Most accounts atttribute this to the fact that the young Reynolds was not considered (at that early stage in her career) to have a strong enough voice. For information on this, see the following websites: http://www.classicimages.com/1998/november98/idibthee.html; http://www.clarkson.edu/~fbailey/lf373/2-18.html.

5   Chion draws a comparable analogy between the fog and the female voice in his discussion of John Carpenter's horror film *The Fog* (1979) (1999: 119).

6   This emphasis on the capacity of the individual to bring about a sense of change and self-empowerment can also be contrasted with the mood of resignation embodied in *Show Boat*'s song 'Old Man River'. The embracing of Buddhism by Anna Mae thereby enables the film to

reject the convention (inherent in certain traditional white representations of black culture) of using more orthodox forms of religion like
Christianity to bind blacks into a passive acceptance of their lot.

7   *Stormy Weather* (Andrew L. Stone, 1943), *Broadway Melody of 1940*
(Norman Taurog, 1939) and *Cabaret* (Bob Fosse, 1972) are examples of
other musicals where the proposal or prospect of marriage also brings
with it the expectation and pressure that the woman will give up her
independent performing career, but in these films (unlike in *White
Christmas*) it is met with varying degrees of resistance.

8   On the ways in which Judy Garland's own particular associations with
suffering and endurance have been understood by gay men, see Dyer
1986: 141–56.

BIBLIOGRAPHY

Essential reading

Altman, R. (1987) *The American Film Musical*. London: British Film
Institute.
A formidably rigorous study that, emerging out of the structuralist
phase of film studies, seeks to offer a systematic account of the
musical's defining features and ideological operations. It explores the
ways in which the musical is structured in terms of a dual-focus narrative (involving the formation of the couple) and categorises the genre
according to three main forms: the fairytale musical, the show musical
and the folk musical.
_____ (ed.) (1981) *Genre: The Musical*. London and New York: Routledge
and Kegan Paul.
An invaluable anthology that contains some of the most important
early seminal pieces of writing on the musical.
Babington, B. and P. W. Evans (1985) *Blue Skies and Silver Linings: Aspects
of the Hollywood Musical*. Manchester: Manchester University Press.
A thoughtful, intelligent study that is notable for offering detailed readings of a number of individual musicals. In covering several different
types of musical from the 1930s period through to the 1970s, it conveys a strong sense of the diversity and richness of the genre.
Cohan, S. (ed.) (2002) *Hollywood Musicals: The Film Reader*. London and
New York: Routledge.
A useful collection of previously published and newly commissioned
articles, this book covers the musical's importance as a generic form,

the role played by spectacle in the genre's construction of gender and sexual difference, the musical's appeal to gay audiences and its construction of itself as a dominantly white entertainment form.

Dyer, R. (1981 [1977]) 'Entertainment and Utopia', in R. Altman (ed.) *Genre: The Musical*. London and New York: Routledge and Kegan Paul, 176–89.

An extremely influential article that explores the ways in which the musical functions as a utopian form of entertainment. It outlines the main categories of the utopian sensibility and examines how these can be understood as responding to needs and inadequacies in society.

Feuer, J. (1993) *The Hollywood Musical* (second edition). Hampshire and London: Macmillan.

A lucid and accessible study, this book investigates the idea that the Hollywood musical is a form of mass entertainment that seeks to pass itself off as folk art. This second edition (the first edition was published by the British Film Institute in 1982) contains an interesting Postscript wherein the author reflects critically on her original study and considers how more recent developments both in the musical and in film studies as a whole may prompt certain qualifications to her original thesis.

Malone, J. (1996) *Steppin' on the Blues: The Visible Rhythms of African American Dance*. Urbana and Chicago: University of Illinois Press.

Offers an illuminating insight into the history of black dance in America. It explores how the form has evolved from the days of slavery and examines its vital importance to African American culture. Both this and Marshall and Jean Stearns' book *Jazz Dance* (see Secondary Reading) provide an invaluable background to the study of black performances in the Hollywood musical and are also helpful in understanding the broader influence that African American forms of music and dance have had on the genre.

Marshall, B. and R. Stilwell (eds) (2000) *Musicals: Hollywood and Beyond*. Exeter: Intellect Books.

Offers a very useful collection of essays on topics relating to music, race and individual star performers. Also includes contributions on aspects of the musical in European cinema.

Neale, S. (2000) *Genre and Hollywood*. London: Routledge.

The section on 'Musicals' (104–12) offers a very useful general overview of academic work on the genre while also helping to situate a study of the musical within the broader context of genre studies as a whole.

Secondary reading

Aaron, M. (2000) 'Hardly Chazans: *Yentl* and the Singing Jew', in B. Marshall and R. Stilwell (eds) *Musicals: Hollywood and Beyond*. Exeter: Intellect Books, 125–31.

Arbuthnot, L. and G. Seneca (1982) 'Pre-text and Text in *Gentlemen Prefer Blondes*', in S. Cohan (ed.) (2002) *Hollywood Musicals: The Film Reader*. London and New York: Routledge, 77–85.

Bailey, F. *'Singin' in the Rain*: Ideas for Discussion', Online. Available at: http://www.clarkson.edu/~fbailey/lf373/2-18.html.

Baron, E. T. (1994) 'Deriding the Voice of Jeanette MacDonald: Notes on Psychoanalysis and the American Film Musical', in L. C. Dunn & N. A. Jones (eds) *Embodied Voices: Representing Female Sexuality in Western Culture*. Cambridge, New York and Melbourne: Cambridge University Press.

Bogle, D. (1994) *Toms, Coons, Mulattoes, Mammies, and Bucks: An Interpretive History of Blacks in American Films*. Oxford: Roundhouse.

Braun, E. (2004) (revised edition) *Doris Day*. London: Orion Books.

Britton, A. (1995) *Katharine Hepburn: Star as Feminist*. London: Studio Vista. (See section on Fred Astaire, 128–33.)

Chion, M. (1999) *The Voice in Cinema*, edited and translated by Claudia Gorbman. New York: Columbia University Press.

Clarke, J., D. Simmonds and M. Merke (1980) 'Move Over Misconceptions: Doris Day Reappraised', BFI Dossier No. 4. London: British Film Institute.

____ (1982) 'Doris Day Case Study: Stars and Exhibition' in C. Gledhill (ed.) *Star Signs*. London: British Film Institute.

Cohan, S. (1993) '"Feminizing" the Song-and-Dance Man: Fred Astaire and the Spectacle of Masculinity', in S. Cohan (ed.) (2002) *Hollywood Musicals: The Film Reader*. London and New York: Routledge, 87–101.

Delamater. J. (1978) *Dance in the Hollywood Musical*. Ann Arbor: UMI Research Press.

Du Maurier, G. (1894) *Trilby*. Oxford World's Classics edition published in 1998, Oxford and New York: Oxford University Press.

Dyer, R. (1986) *Heavenly Bodies: Film Stars and Society*. Hampshire and London: Macmillan.

____ (1991 [1980]) '*A Star is Born* and the Construction of Authenticity', in C. Gledhill (ed.) *Stardom: Industry of Desire*. London: Routledge,

132–40.

____ (2000 [1995]) 'The Colour of Entertainment', in B. Marshall & R. Stilwell (eds) *Musicals: Hollywood and Beyond*. Exeter: Intellect Books, 23–30.

Fascinatin' Rhythm: The Story of Tap (2001). Omnibus BBC documentary (broadcast on 24 February 2001).

Fischer, L. (1981 [1976]) 'The Image of Woman as Image: The Optical Politics of *Dames*', in R. Altman (ed.) *Genre: The Musical*. London and New York: Routledge and Kegan Paul, 71–84.

Frank, R. E. (1994) (revised edition) *Tap! The Greatest Tap Dance Stars and Their Stories, 1900–1955*. New York: De Capo Press.

Gallafent, E. (2000) *Astaire and Rogers*. Moffat: Cameron and Hollis.

Hill, C. V. (2000) *Brotherhood in Rhythm: The Jazz Tap Dancing of the Nicholas Brothers*. New York: Oxford University Press.

Hoberman, J. (1993) *42nd Street*. London: British Film Institute.

Kemp, P. (2000) 'How Do You Solve a "Problem" Like Maria von Poppins?', in B. Marshall and R. Stilwell (eds) (2000) *Musicals: Hollywood and Beyond*. Exeter: Intellect Books, 55–61.

Kenney, E. J. (ed.) (1998) *Metamorphoses* by Ovid. Trans. E. J. Melville. Oxford World Classics series. Oxford: Oxford University Press.

Kramer, P. (2000) '"A Cutie With More Than Beauty": Audrey Hepburn, the Hollywood Musical and *Funny Face*', in B. Marshall and R. Stilwell (eds) *Musicals: Hollywood and Beyond*. Exeter: Intellect Books, 62–9.

Kreuger, M. (1988) 'Some Words about *Show Boat* by Miles Kreuger', in liner notes to John McGlinn's recording of the music to the show. Available on CD from EMI Records (issue no: 7491082).

Laing, H. (2000) 'Emotion By Numbers: Music, Song and the Musical', in B. Marshall and R. Stilwell (eds) (2000) *Musicals: Hollywood and Beyond*. Exeter: Intellect Books, 5–13.

Lippe, R. (1986) 'Gender and Destiny: George Cukor's *A Star is Born*', *CineAction!*, Winter, 46–57.

McPherson, T. (2003) *Reconstructing Dixie*. Durham and London: Duke University Press.

MacKinnon, K. (2000) '"I Keep Wishing I Were Somewhere Else": Space and Fantasies of Freedom in the Hollywood Musical', in B. Marshall & R. Stilwell (eds) *Musicals: Hollywood and Beyond*. Exeter: Intellect Books, 40–6.

Mellencamp, P. (1995) 'Sexual Economics: *Gold Diggers of 1933*', in

S. Cohan (ed.) (2002) *Hollywood Musicals: The Film Reader*. London and New York: Routledge, 65–76.

Minnelli, V. with H. Arce (1974) *I Remember It Well*. New York, London and Toronto: Samuel French.

Moseley, R. (2002) *Growing Up With Audrey Hepburn*. Manchester: Manchester University Press.

Mulvey, L. (1999) 'Now You Has Jazz: The Innovators 1920–1930', *Sight and Sound*, 9, 5, 16–18.

My Fair Lady: "Wouldn't it be Loverly" (2001). Omnibus BBC documentary (broadcast on 10 March 2001).

Naremore, J. (1988) *Acting in the Cinema*. Berkeley, Los Angeles and London: University of California Press.

_____ (1993) *The Films of Vincente Minnelli*. Cambridge: Cambridge University Press.

Rogin, M. (1996) *Blackface, White Noise: Jewish Immigrants in the Hollywood Melting Pot*. Berkeley, Los Angeles and London: University of California Press.

Shaw, B. (1912) *Pygmalion*, reprinted in J. Fisher (ed.) (1991). Singapore: Longman.

Smith, S. (2000) *Hitchcock: Suspense, Humour and Tone*. London: British Film Institute (see section on Music, 104–15).

Stanfield, P. (2000) 'From the Vulgar to the Refined: American Vernacular and Blackface Minstrelsy in *Showboat*', in B. Marshall & R. Stilwell (eds) *Musicals: Hollywood and Beyond*. Exeter: Intellect Books, 147–56.

Stearns, M. and J. Stearns (1968) *Jazz Dance: The Story of American Vernacular Dance*. New York: De Capo Press.

Thomas, D. (1990) '*Blonde Venus*', *Movie*, 34/35, 7–15.

Turner, T. with K. Loder (1986) *I, Tina*. London: Penguin.

Wagner, L. (1998) '"I Dub Thee": A Guide to the Great Voice Doubles', Online. Available at: http://www.classicimages.com/1998/november98/idibthee.html.

Wollen, P. (1992) *Singin' in the Rain*. London: British Film Institute.

Wood, R. (1979) 'Never Never Change, Always Gonna Dance', *Film Comment* (September/October), 29–31.

_____ (1981 [1975]) 'Art and Ideology: Notes on *Silk Stockings*', in R. Altman (ed.) *Genre: The Musical*. London and New York: Routledge and Kegan Paul, 58–69.

_____ (1986) 'Minnelli's *Madame Bovary*', *CineAction!* (December), 75–80.

INDEX

Music in Film
Soundtracks and Synergy
Pauline Reay

2004
£12.99 (pbk) 1-903364-65-5

Music in Film: Soundtracks and Synergy discusses a broad range of films – from classical Hollywood through to American independents and European art films – and offers a brief history of the development of music in film from the silent era to the present day. In particular, this book explores how music operates as a narrative device, and also emotionally and culturally. By focusing on the increasing synergy between film and music texts, it includes an extended case study of *Magnolia* as a film script which developed from a pop song. Emphasis is also placed on the divide between the 'high culture' of the orchestral score and the 'low culture' of the pop song.

Pauline Reay is a lecturer in Film and Media Studies at various UK educational institutions, with a background in the music industry.

'A thorough overview of the major developments in mainstream film music, this introduction develops into a welcome and much-needed focus on the pop score and soundtrack with excellent and original choices of case study films and performers.'
– David Butler, University of Manchester

Soundscape

The School of Sound Lectures
1998–2001

Edited by Larry Sider

2003
£15.99 (pbk) 1-903364-59-0
£45.00 (hbk) 1-903364-68-X

The School of Sound is a unique annual event exploring the use of sound in film, which has attracted practitioners, academics and artists from around the world. *Soundscape: The School of Sound Lectures, 1998–2001* is the first compendium of the event's presentations that investigate the modern soundtrack and the ways sound combines with image in both art and entertainment. The many contributors include directors David Lynch and Mike Figgis; Oscar-winning sound designer Walter Murch (*Apocalypse Now*); composer Carter Burwell (Coen Brothers); theorists Laura Mulvey and Michel Chion; critic Peter Wollen; filmmakers Mani Kaul and Peter Kubelka; music producer Manfred Eicher and poet Tom Paulin.

Larry Sider is Director of the School of Sound, Head of Production at the National Film and Television School and lectures on film sound throughout Europe. He has been a film editor and sound designer for 25 years and has contributed to *Filmwaves, Framework, Vertigo* and several professional periodicals.

'These essays comprise an insider's perspective on the creative process and contain anecdotes that illustrate the specific challenges and problems that one encounters in developing aesthetically and culturally rich audio-visual experiences.'
– *Senses of Cinema*

Popular Music and Film

Edited by Ian Inglis

2003
£14.99 (pbk) 1-903364-71-X
£45.00 (hbk) 1-903364-72-8

The growing presence of popular music in film is one of the most exciting areas of contemporary Film Studies. Written by a range of international specialists, this collection includes case studies on *Sliding Doors*, *Topless Women Talk About Their Lives*, *The Big Chill* and *Moulin Rouge*, considering the work of populist musicians such as the Beatles, Jimi Hendrix and Sting.

Contributors to the volume include Robb Wright, Lesley Vize, Phil Powrie, Anno Mungen, Anaheid Kassabian, Lauren Anderson, Antti-Ville Karja, K. J. Donnelly, Lee Barron, Melissa Carey Michael Hannan and Jaap Kooijman.

Ian Inglis is Senior Lecturer in Sociology at the University of Northumbria. He is the editor of *The Beatles, Popular Music and Society: A Thousand Voices* (2000) and has published widely on music and cinema.

CLOSE UP #1

Fimmaker's Choices
The Pop Song in Film
Reading Buffy

edited by John Gibbs and Douglas Pye

October 2005
£18.99 pbk 1-904764-57-6
£50.00 hbk 1-904764-66-5

CLOSE UP is an innovative and accessible new annual series devoted to the close analysis of film and television. Each volume will contain three extended individual studies linked by a concern to explore in detail the decisions that go into the making of films or television programmes. These choices – from setting and performance to camera position and movement, from lighting and colour to editing and the multiple possibilities of sound – create a film's form and determine its meanings. It is this rich texture that engages us as spectators but has often been overlooked in film theory and criticism. Each study in the series will root its argument in particular choices made by filmmakers, providing sustained analysis of sequences and moments and engaging with wider issues in the field from this firm basis in textual detail.

One of the individual studies in *CLOSE UP* #1 is *The Pop Song in Film* by Ian Garwood. This offers a series of detailed interpretations of moments in films where the pop song adopts a decisive storytelling role. The study focuses on both on-screen musical performances and the use of the song as a kind of musical voiceover. It features close commentary on examples ranging from the Frank Sinatra star-vehicle musical *Young at Heart* (1954) to the opening of Quentin Tarantino's *Jackie Brown* (1997).